The Importance of Being Ernie

The Importance
of Being Ernie

From *My Three Sons* to *Mad Men*,
a Hollywood Survivor Tells All

BARRY LIVINGSTON

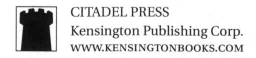

CITADEL PRESS
Kensington Publishing Corp.
WWW.KENSINGTONBOOKS.COM

CITADEL PRESS BOOKS are published by

Kensington Publishing Corp.
119 West 40th Street
New York, NY 10018

ISBN-13: 978-0-8065-4341-3
ISBN-10: 0-8065-4341-8

First Citadel hardcover printing: November 2011
First trade paperback edition: March 2023

10 9 8 7 6 5 4 3 2 1

Printed in the United States of America

Electronic edition:

ISBN-13: 978-0-8065-3525-8 (e-book)
ISBN-10: 0-8065-3525-3 (e-book)

There are so many people—family, friends, and colleagues—who I owe a debt of gratitude, for enriching my career and my life. To them I offer my heartfelt thanks. One person deserves so much more, my wife, Karen. She has been my touchstone for over three decades. Her patience, wisdom, humor, counsel, and love elevate me in every way. To her I dedicate this book.

Contents

Foreword

by Stanley Livingston

My brother Barry and I have shared a lifetime together. We shared a bedroom growing up. We broke into show business together. We shared a ride to work together. We shared a dressing room. We shared credit, appearing in some of television's most memorable shows together. We share a legacy in showbiz together.

Although there exists a little thing called nepotism in show business, I have to set the record straight. My brother has always been his own man (even as a child). Each and every television and movie part he landed—in an extraordinary fifty-plus-year career—he fought for and won because of his determination as a person and his undeniable talents as an actor.

I watched my brother wisely re-invent himself as an actor after *My Three Sons* ended in 1972. Most actors would have packed it in and started selling insurance or used cars. Not Barry. He headed off to work on the stages of Broadway and Off-Broadway, and began his career and life anew.

I watched my brother go through some challenging moments as well as some high points as an actor—and as a human being. I never heard him complain about the hardships or brag about his good fortune. My brother is stoic and relentless. He always stays the course.

Along the way, my brother found love and marriage, and became the quintessential family man. As a busy working actor, he has never put his career in front of his family. Sometimes I think my brother is "Steve Douglas" or "Ozzie Nelson" reincarnate. He has more than a picture-perfect home life. He has the "real deal"—a wife, a son, and a daughter who are truly loving and not afraid to express it.

This book is a new venture for my brother and will show another side of his many talents—his amazing gift as a writer. Of course, I already knew that. But you are about to find out. My brother can spin a yarn and has a dazzling way with words. *The Importance of Being Ernie* proves that.

For my reel- (and real-) life brother I have only love, admiration, and respect. I'm not sure we ever had a real fight. We have never been rivals—only supporters of each other's endeavors and dreams. The truth is if Barry weren't my brother, he'd be my best friend. Can a brother be a best friend? I'm sure of it!

With Love . . .
Stanley Livingston
Los Angeles
March 2011

PROLOGUE

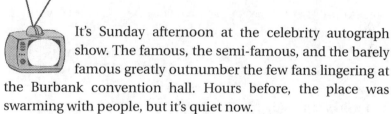 It's Sunday afternoon at the celebrity autograph show. The famous, the semi-famous, and the barely famous greatly outnumber the few fans lingering at the Burbank convention hall. Hours before, the place was swarming with people, but it's quiet now.

Retired elderly stars sit at tables and stare blankly into space. People are finished buying their 8 × 10 photos, publicity pictures of them from an old film or a classic TV series shot decades ago. They looked young and vital back then. Most of these actors are unrecognizable now; wrinkles and hair loss have overwhelmed them. Other aged familiar faces in the room thought they could defy aging with plastic surgery. They've turned into mummified versions of their former selves. Not a good look.

The autograph show has another class of celebrity: the middle-aged thespians. They're divided into two groups. The first type in this category hasn't acted professionally for years, because they quit the business. The industry rejection was too painful. They're now content to bask in the praise of loyal fans instead of getting kicked in the groin by Hollywood on a regular basis. Smart. The second type is a more complicated breed: they are the stubborn veteran performers who've remained in the game, still chasing acting jobs in Hollywood like they were hungry rookies. There are only a few of these crazies at the show. I'm part of that odd little sect of masochists.

My table is also covered with 8 × 10 pictures from past projects I've acted in. Most of them were taken a long, long time ago, when puberty had just kicked in and I was smiling like a Cheshire cat. Who knew that one future day I'd be selling these photos for twenty bucks a pop? Pretty surreal. In fact, the only thing more surreal is when someone actually buys one. That hasn't happened in hours, though.

The clock on the wall says it's three o'clock, two more hours until closing time. I've officially entered the *Twilight Zone*, when there's nothing to do except gaze at your peers . . . and wonder.

On my left is Richard Dreyfus, star of *Jaws, Close Encounters of a Third Kind*, and a few other bona fide movie classics. During the lull, Richard is counting a fistful of bills, twenties I'm guessing. He rakes in the bucks at these events on the weekends and works in prestigious film projects on the weekdays. On my right is Jay North who played Dennis in *Dennis the Menace*, the 1960s TV series. Jay is counting a tall stack of unsold photos and looking glum. One of these two actors is an Oscar winner and the other is employed as a prison guard somewhere in Florida. I'm sure you know which one is which. What do I have in common with these two guys? We were all successful child actors.

If you didn't already know me by name, my early renown came from *My Three Sons*, a 1960s TV series that ran for twelve years. I was the youngest "son," Ernie Douglas, a prototype nerd, which is how one excited fan once described me. I like that label, especially since fellow nerds like Bill Gates, founder of Microsoft, and Mark Zuckerberg, creator of Facebook, now rule the planet.

I can't help comparing my life to guys like Richard Dreyfus and Jay North. Our journeys have gone to such different spectrums of success. Richard climbed to the pinnacle of acting acclaim while Jay's career plummeted to obscurity. Currently,

I'm somewhere in the middle, not an Oscar winner but not pa-
trolling Cell Block 11, either.

I am a character actor who works on a regular basis. I've
recently appeared in high-profile films with Robert Downey Jr.,
Katie Holmes, and Adam Sandler, and been seen on such
acclaimed TV shows as *Madman, Big Love, Desperate House-
wives,* and *Two and a Half Men.* No small achievement in my
mind, because it hasn't always been this way. There was a pro-
longed, painful dip in my fortunes and self-esteem after the first
massive wave of fame disappeared. That was about four
decades ago. I had to fight my way back to become credible
again. "Reinventing yourself" is the term people in the film industry use for such transformations. It sounds simple, but nothing is *simple* in Hollywood.

People ask me: Why do some child actors lose everything—
their money, their reputations, even their lives? Conversely, a
few child stars have beaten the odds and gone on to great success as adult performers. There has to be more to it than luck
and talent. It's a tricky question, and the answer involves parents, siblings, friends, and life experiences, the good, the bad,
and the embarrassing. Sometimes you've got to go back to your
beginning to understand the ending. It's been a long, twisting
roller-coaster journey. This is what I remember about the
ride . . .

CHAPTER 1

Birth of a Nerd

I was born in Hollywood, December 17, 1953. My first home was located in the heart of town on Formosa Avenue, north of Santa Monica Boulevard. This is the city that gave birth to world-famous studios, Paramount, Columbia, and 20th Century-Fox, and we were living a half block away from one of the best dream factories, the Samuel Goldwyn Studios.

One of my earliest memories is walking with my mother past the Goldwyn lot, a fortress-like compound with high walls and guarded gates. I was just three years old and fascinated by the place. It reminded me of a fort, specifically the cavalry outpost that I saw on my favorite TV show, *Rin-Tin-Tin*. The series featured Rusty, a young army mascot, and his beautiful German shepherd, Rin-Tin-Tin. I wanted a life like Rusty's, living in a fort with a really cool dog.

I was in awe of the studio's big iron gates, which would open up for only a few lucky people. I couldn't help but wonder, What could be happening behind those massive barriers that was so important that it required guards to keep out the common rabble? My mom said she'd heard that the Samuel Goldwyn Studio is where they actually filmed *Rin-Tin-Tin*, and then I understood: important activities really were going on inside the "fort." I wanted to go inside, badly.

Without a doubt, my parents stoked my interest in movies. Not intentionally, though. I absorbed cinema history through osmosis because my mom and dad talked about it with such love and knowledge. They owned two theaters in Baltimore during the 1930s and 1940s, and saw every film ever released in those decades, over and over. The film bug infected their blood, and when I was born, it became part of my DNA, too.

According to family lore, my dad inherited the theaters from his father who was a bookie, who acquired the cinemas as pay-off from a debtor. The story of how my parents met is even more colorful. My dad hired my mother to work at one of his theaters located on The Block, an infamously seedy part of town. Her job wasn't ticket-taker or usher. My mom was a "fan dancer" like the famous stripper, Gypsy Rose Lee. Not your average mom and pop.

Back in the era, the theater business was open night and day, presenting films and live entertainment. There were multiple showings of the A movie—the main event—and the B movie, making it a double feature. They also screened newsreels, short subjects, and cartoons, and live entertainers performed between the films. Comedians, singers, and of course, fan-dancers would trot out to charm the rowdy crowd, mostly troops on leave and the local down-and-outers.

By all accounts, the routines of fan-dancers were tame compared to the nude pole-dancers of today. Mom dressed in a one-piece bathing suit and hid behind giant peacock feathers, strutting around the stage and flashing a little skin to the beat of a drum. It's creepy to think of your mother doing such things, but it's kind of cool, too, for its shock value if nothing else.

After the war ended, a little invention called television got very popular, and attendance at the movies nose-dived. The independent theaters couldn't compete. They became dying relics of a lost world and faded away like the dinosaurs . . . and fan-dancers. In 1949, my parents unloaded the family business and headed for Hollywood, hoping for a new start.

My mom and dad never lost their love of films, though. After watching a movie, my parents would rattle off the names of practically every actor we'd just seen. Not just the stars, they knew the names of every supporting actor, too.

My dad would say things like, "Bogart was okay, but Sidney Greenstreet stole the movie."

My mom would counter, "Honestly, I think Ward Bond is sexier than Bogart!"

Ward Bond? Sidney Greenstreet? Better than Bogart? Their list of unheralded actors went on and on: Frank Morgan, Edward Everett Horton, Billie Burke, Sam Jaffe, William Bendix. Some of these actors were fat, bug eyed, or jolly, while others were frail, pompous, or morose. The one thing they all had in common: *character.* You could tell my parents loved these guys for their oddball personalities and quirky looks. That impressed me. Being a character actor seemed like something to aspire to.

During our first few years in Hollywood, we weren't living like ex–movie moguls from Baltimore. It was a paycheck above poverty level. Our rented two-bedroom cottage on Formosa Avenue was so shabby and old that it nearly collapsed in an earthquake that hit Long Beach, a hundred miles away.

We were eating dinner, and the ground started to sway. My parents, East Coast "rookies," were kind of giddy at first. The shaking wasn't as bad as they'd heard. Then the quake grew stronger as the walls buckled and light fixtures swayed.

My mom hissed, "Hilliard, what's happening? What are we supposed to do?"

Nobody knew what was coming next. My dad finally said, "I think we're supposed to get in a doorway."

I don't recall any of us moving an inch. We just sat in our breakfast nook, peering through a big picture window, half expecting to see a swarm of locusts or a biblical flood. It was pitch-black outside, and I saw my family's ghostly reflections vibrating in the shaking glass. As the ground settled, I sensed that mysterious forces were loose in the world. It was unpredictable, scary, and kind of fun, too.

The fun ended fast, though, once we saw that our shack was shaken off its foundation. The landlord was in no hurry to fix it, either, and our future slipped from bleak to dire. The pressure to rescue the family was on my dad. My mother often said he was a genius. *Troubled* genius would have been a better description.

My father suffered from a paralyzing inferiority complex, perhaps the result of too much pressure applied by his parents, Jewish immigrants. It may sound like a cliché, but all their children had to be high achievers . . . or die. My dad certainly had the potential to excel; he entered NYU at age sixteen as the designated family lawyer. After four years, he finished the law program but was too young to take the bar exam. He decided to switch majors and become a psychologist, another parental-approved profession. Not long after that, he focused on foreign languages, becoming fluent in French and Spanish.

My dad devised a pretty clever plan: keep switching majors so you never get a degree in anything; that way you'll never have to get a real job and be judged.

Eventually, my father found a better way to escape everyone's expectations. When his dad died, he abandoned college altogether and assumed the job of running the movie theaters. With one ingenious stroke, he became a hero for saving the family business, while forever avoiding a college graduation day. Thus, he became the "promising genius" in perpetuity. It was the bane of his life.

Despite all his hang-ups, my mother never gave up hope on my dad and a brighter future. She had met him when she was sixteen, after running away from her dreary home in Beaver Falls, Pennsylvania. He seemed like a knight in shining armor, with his good looks and sterling academic reputation. She was going to be the "woman behind the great man." Over time, when she realized she'd invested in a flawed "diamond," her disappointment grew.

Now that our earthquake-damaged house in Hollywood was tilting like the leaning Tower of Pisa, my mother wanted the "great man" to get off his butt and do something about it. She wanted action, and fast. Doing anything, let alone doing it fast, wasn't my father's style. Apathy was his middle name. That might explain why he chose to work as a salesman at Charles Furniture in South Central Los Angeles, a job he held his entire life.

My dad inspected our battered home and seemed unfazed. Even the hole in our living room ceiling wasn't too bad. He said, "Let's just stay here and try to get the landlord to repair the place."

My mother flipped. She said, "If you want to stay here, with the cracked walls and hole in the roof, you are nuts! I'll be god-damned if I'm staying!" She swore like a drunken sailor. Most ex–fan dancers do.

Somehow my mom scraped up the money to rent a dinky duplex on Wilcox Avenue in Hollywood and even arranged for movers to haul our secondhand furniture. As we vacated the shack on Formosa, my sullen dad followed us like a sad puppy, tail between his legs.

We didn't live in our new duplex for very long, though. The place turned out to be a bigger dump than the shack. Worse yet, it was infested with roaches. This was no big deal to my dad; nothing a couple cans of Raid couldn't fix. Mom flipped, again, and we hauled our meager belongings across the street into our new apartment home on Wilcox. This turned out to be a great move because the building was crawling with kids. This is where my life really got interesting.

CHAPTER 2

Wild on Wilcox

 Hours after moving into our apartment home, my older brother, Stan, and I made a slew of new pals: Ray Canada, oldest kid in the building and de facto leader; the two obese brothers, Russell and John Hare; Alan Nickoletti; and Gary DiMeo. The street was alive with handball games in the parking lot, rubber-band gunfights, and knuckle-bruising swordfights with sticks.

Music echoed through the building, too. Ray Canada's family blared Italian operas; the Hares were big Four Seasons fans; and Alan Nickoletti's dad, a music teacher, played polka tunes non-stop on his accordion. Old man Nickoletti even sold my mom a used upright piano and a ukulele, hoping to drum up some students. We never took any lessons, but that didn't stop my brother and me from banging on the piano like a couple of deranged Little Richards.

Basically, the neighborhood was poor working class. Because everyone's parents worked all day, the kids living at the apartment building ran wild in an unsupervised jungle. It's where I honed my street survival skills, especially while pulling our juvenile pranks.

One of our gang's favorite stunts was bombarding passing cars with water balloons. On more than one occasion, an enraged driver would hop out of his vehicle and chase us. Being the youngest, I was always at the rear of the pack, just out of reach of some cursing, sopping-wet maniac.

Another favorite practical joke was to mold a hand out of clay, paint the wrist blood red, like the whole meathook had just been severed, and attach it to somebody's doorknob. The real fun began when somebody, usually me, would pound on the door and run away. From our hiding place, we'd watch some unsuspecting old biddy open the door and discover the gruesome bloody mitt. If she screamed, so much the better. Mission accomplished.

Our gang also loved combing local construction sites for metal pipes to be used as swords and metal slugs from electrical outlet boxes. The round slugs were like real coins and could be used to buy baseball cards or candy among the local kids.

Occasionally, our raiding party encountered real danger on our treasure hunts. On one such adventure a rottweiler security dog cornered Stan, Ray Canada, and me on the third floor of a partially built apartment building. The only way to escape was to jump, which is what Stan did. He landed in a huge pile of sand twenty feet below and laughed like a madman, thrilled by his daring aerial escape. He waved for me to join him, but I couldn't do it. The snapping dog was scary as hell, but the thought of falling three stories was more terrifying.

A crusty old security guard appeared on the scene, cursing and waving his flashlight like a hot-white laser beam. I knew I *had* to jump now, but I still couldn't budge. Our gang's sworn motto was based on the Marines' credo, "Never leave one of your own behind." With that solemn vow in mind, Ray Canada latched on to my arm and yanked me off the building's scaffolding.

I was suddenly surrounded by a silky, soft nothingness. As the song says: "*Falling feels like flying . . . for a little while.*" I landed hard on the mountain of wet sand, which knocked the air out of my lungs. I gasped to catch my breath, but thankfully nothing was broken. We rolled off the hill and ran for our lives as the security guard and dog both howled at us from above.

Halloween was also an especially fun time on Wilcox Avenue. It was a little dangerous, too, because roving gangs of trick-or-treaters were armed with pirate swords and fake rifles with hard plastic bayonets. A squad of teenage G.I. Joe's pursued me five city blocks to steal my booty of candy, which I refused to hand over. I thought I was going to get away, too, as I scaled a chain-link fence. Unfortunately, my Zorro cape got caught on the metal barbs at the top of the fence. I hung there, in my black mask and beautiful gaucho hat, and took a beating like a piñata until some adults rescued me.

The local city park at Cahuenga and Santa Monica was another childhood hangout. It had a huge, overly chlorinated swimming pool that my dad called the Cold Pool. Even in the dead of summer, the water felt like we were flailing around in the North Sea.

Our neighborhood gang was also within striking distance of Hollywood Boulevard and its dozens of movie theaters. Most Saturdays we'd head up there to catch a triple-feature of horror flicks, movies like *The Brain Eaters*, *A Bucket of Blood*, and *Pit and the Pendulum*. Anything that starred Vincent Price was a must-see. Also, the Ray Harryhausen epics like *Jason and the Argonauts* and *The Seventh Voyage of Sinbad* were mind-boggling cinematic achievements in our book.

Our favorite old movie palace was the Pix Theater. It had a great balcony that was perfect for bombarding the patrons seated below with candy. Every time a movie veered into a boring love scene, Good & Plenty licorice would fly. It was during one of our visits to the Pix to see *The Raven* that I became aware of a portly, bug-eyed actor named Peter Lorre. He was the geekiest actor I'd ever seen *starring* in a movie. I was impressed.

I'd seen other oddball characters on TV like Wally Cox in *Mr. Peepers* and Froggy from *The Little Rascals*. There was something about Peter Lorre, though, a quirky charisma that nobody else possessed. His sad round face made him look like a wide-eyed Boston terrier. You couldn't take your eyes off him. I also found that I could mimic his nasal eastern European dialect, which really scored points with my pals. That peer group approval surprised and pleased me. It opened my eyes to something amazing: I possessed a talent. Who knew? An acting seed was sown.

Another actor who made a big impression on me was Vincent Price, Lorre's acting partner in a number of Roger Corman horror films. Price was such a refined and giddy sadist. Come to think of it, he was a pretty odd duck, too. Perhaps the term "elegant nerd," would be the best way to describe him.

Price starred in a film that I saw over and over again, forever scarring my young psyche. The flick was called *House on Haunted Hill*. While Price scared the hell out of everyone on screen, the theater owner rigged a skeleton on a wire and pulled it above the audience during a few tense moments, adding to the terror. The movie industry was desperate to lure audiences away from their TVs, and no campy trick was ruled out.

Naturally, kids who'd already seen the film came armed and prepared for the skeleton on their second viewing. As soon as the bag of bones came flying out from the theater's wings, it was pelted by a barrage of Milk Duds, Rollo Bars, and, of course, Good & Plenty. The poor people seeing the movie for the first time got two shocks: the terrifying entrance of the flying skeleton as well as a hailstorm of hard candies. Good times.

We found another activity on the boulevard after the city installed a new sidewalk, the Hollywood Walk of Fame. Once the concrete dried, it was slick as ice and great for roller-skating. My brother and I would head up there late at night accompanied by our huge sheep dog, Patchy. We'd put on our skates, attach two leashes to the dog's collar, and yell, "*Mush*," just like we'd seen Sergeant Preston do with his dog, Yukon King, on another TV favorite, *Sergeant Preston of the Yukon*.

Patchy would haul ass down the boulevard like a galloping Clydesdale, and we'd roll right behind her, trying to keep our balance. If one of your steel skate wheels hit even the smallest pebble, it would stop on a dime and you'd go face forward, getting dragged across the "stars in concrete" by our sprinting dog.

My first public school was at the Vine Street Elementary School. Besides learning the alphabet and basic math, we were also taught to do "drop and cover" exercises in case the Russians attacked Hollywood with an A-bomb. My teacher was deadly serious about it, too. She'd be facing the chalkboard, calmly scribbling an arithmetic problem, and suddenly whirl around to face the class.

"Drop!" she'd scream with her eyes as big as mushroom clouds.

Having been conditioned to instantly respond to her command, we'd fall out of our chairs and cram our five-year-old bodies under our wooden tables with our heads to the floor, butts in the air. This was supposed to protect us from the inevitable hellacious nuclear fireball. It was scary as hell but kind of thrilling, too, and a welcome break from adding and subtracting.

I was only five years old, but I walked home after school every day, heading north up Vine Street. Once I hit Santa Monica Blvd., I was instructed to turn left and head west toward Wilcox, where I'd make a right and then skedaddle home. My mother insisted that this was the only route I should take home. I was to stay on the main roads for safety reasons. I finally asked why it was so much safer on the big streets.

She kneeled down on one knee to get on my eye level, held me by the shoulders to focus my attention, and said, "Perverts are lurking on the side streets just waiting to molest little boys."

I stayed off the side streets like they were home to zombies. Still do. My mother always had crude but effective ways of making her points.

Unfortunately, my route home took me right past the home of a flying monster, a giant carpenter bee. I told my mom about my problem, but she was unmoved. Perverts were worse than bees in her mind.

The big, black, hideous flying insect lived in a hole that it had drilled (I just assumed it could drill, being a *carpenter* bee) in a creosote-soaked telephone pole. The buzzing bastard lay in wait every day, like the proverbial troll living under the bridge.

I approached the bee's hole, which oozed a nasty black tar, and I could hear a low vibrating rumble from deep inside. Every day I prayed that I could tiptoe past its lair. No such luck. Just as I passed the pole, its bulbous head would emerge like a creature from one of our beloved monster movies. We'd make eye contact. Its wings would flap in an angry blur, daring me to run . . . and I would, flailing my arms in the air as the giant bee orbited my head like an errant Nazi buzz bomb. After sprinting in sheer terror for a city block or so, I'd either outrun the damn thing or it would lose interest in messing with my head . . . until the next day.

Evenings at home were mostly spent right in front of the TV, literally, sitting about two feet away from the screen. My mother, ever the oracle of wisdom and doom, would scream, "Move back . . . or you'll go blind!"

Once again, her warnings were prophetic because I was wearing glasses not long afterward.

I loved to watch a program called *The Million Dollar Movie* because the TV station presented the same film every night for a week, twice a day on Saturdays and Sundays. If it was a Western or a war movie, I'd watch every showing, assuming my mom would let me. She'd usually be sitting right alongside me if the movie starred John Wayne, her favorite actor.

The best of all TV programs was *The Honeymooners*, my dad's favorite show. It was a particular treat to watch because it aired in reruns late at night, around eleven thirty. My brother and I had to have special permission to stay up to watch it. To this day, when I hear *The Honeymooners* theme song and see Jackie Gleason's face appear inside that pale white moon, I get giddy. There was nothing more magical than sharing belly laughs with your family at midnight.

Other than the joy *The Honeymooners* brought to our home, there wasn't a whole lot of laughter between our parents. My dad's lack of drive in the career department and his bouts with depression were driving my mom nuts. Wanting to escape our dreary surroundings, she started taking my brother and me to a swim school up on Hollywood Boulevard, east of Western Avenue. Oddly enough, that place was key to our becoming actors.

CHAPTER 3

Swim School and the Big Break

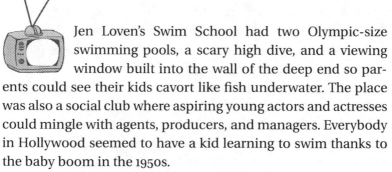 Jen Loven's Swim School had two Olympic-size swimming pools, a scary high dive, and a viewing window built into the wall of the deep end so parents could see their kids cavort like fish underwater. The place was also a social club where aspiring young actors and actresses could mingle with agents, producers, and managers. Everybody in Hollywood seemed to have a kid learning to swim thanks to the baby boom in the 1950s.

My high-spirited mom was soon in the thick of the pool's social whirl. She was making friends with an exciting new group of people, folks like the world-famous trumpeter Jack Sheldon. Jack was married to Jen Loven's daughter, and his hipster friends included guys like comic Lenny Bruce and legendary musician Miles Davis.

My mom befriended a poolside lounge lizard, Sonny Tufts, who was an aging star of B movies. Tufts had long been on the verge of stardom with good supporting roles in *The Seven Year Itch* and *The Virginian*, but his career was stymied by bouts with alcohol. When we first met the bronzed, blond-haired actor, he had just "fallen off the wagon," again. This was after a year of sobriety while Tufts tried to land the role of Jim Bowie in the John Wayne epic, *The Alamo*. When the role went to Richard Widmark, Tufts went back to the "bottle."

Sonny loved gathering the pool kids to sing the Hamm's beer commercial jingle. He'd pound out the song's Indian tom-tom drumbeat with his fist and we'd chirp: *"From the land of sky blue water . . . Hamm's, the beer refreshing, Hamm's, the beer refreshing, Haammmm's!"*

What a great role model for the future child stars of America. Any substance abuse I suffered later, I can blame on him.

The first acting job in my family came about purely by accident while we were at the swim school. Sonny's agent, a lady named Tina Hill, invited a reporter from the *Los Angeles Times* to come to the pool to interview her client and write about the lively social scene. When the reporter arrived, he quickly lost interest in Sonny, who was already crooning the Hamm's beer jingle.

The reporter asked a few of the young swimmers to ride their metal tricycles across the bottom of the pool, underwater. He wanted to take some photos of us through the big underground window that looked into the pool's deep end. This guy was no Ansel Adams, but he knew a good shot when he saw one.

When the photos were printed in the newspaper, they were really eye catching, and a producer of the TV series *Lassie* saw my brother in one of the underwater shots. He realized that Stan resembled Timmy, the little boy character on his show. Their similar looks might solve a big problem he was facing. In an upcoming episode that was to be filmed, Timmy almost drowns in a lake, and the child actor who played the character couldn't swim. Stan was the perfect "stunt double."

The phone rang one evening at our home while the family was gathered around the tube watching *The Ed Sullivan Show.* My mom answered and listened to the producer from *Lassie* inquiring about Stan's availability to do a "drowning" scene. She thought it was a prank and hung up on the guy.

The producer persisted, calling back to tell her that the job paid a few hundred dollars, which was a lot of money in those days. Now my mom became less skeptical and my brother became much more available.

Stan went to work on *Lassie* a few days later and made his acting debut: flailing, splashing, and finally submerging anonymously in some studio pond. It was an odd beginning to a career, but you've got to start somewhere, I suppose, even if it's at the bottom of a pool.

Presto, chango! With one scant appearance on TV, Stan went from swim school tadpole to a professional thespian. Agent Tina Hill smelled money and convinced my mom to let her become his theatrical representative. Tina was a kind of low-level agent. There were no big stars on her roster of clients, just aging has-beens like Sonny Tufts and young newcomers. My brother, obviously, was among the latter.

I accompanied my mom and Stan to the Screen Actor's Guild, the actor's union, and watched him sign up. It was pretty impressive to see him write his squiggly signature on official looking documents, like he was joining the army or buying a car. While we were waiting for Stan to finish, my mother found out a surprising fact: anybody could walk in and join the guild, even if you've never had an acting job. It was an "open" union. Hearing that, my mom had an "ah-ha moment": *If both of my kids were actors, we might make enough money to escape our Wilcox ghetto. Barry should sign up, too."* Bam!

Seconds later, I was scratching my signature on a page full of impossibly tiny print and being inducted into the SAG army of thespians. I had no TV credits, or any talent as far as I knew, except imitating Peter Lorre, but I became an actor that day, whether I liked the idea or not. I liked it.

Immediately, our lives took a turn. Tina Hill started sending us out on job interviews, which dramatically changed my after-school routine. No more bucolic walks home eluding perverts on the side streets or being chased by carpenter bees.

Every day at three o'clock, my mom would be parked in front of my school in our ugly old Nash Rambler, honking and yelling, "Get your ass in the car! Hurry up!"

We were perennially late for an audition, sometimes a Cheerios commercial or bit part on *Dragnet*. We found ourselves speeding across Los Angeles to towns that I never knew existed: Culver City, Burbank, *North* Hollywood! As far as I had figured, there was only Hollywood.

Once we arrived at our destination, my mom, Stan, and I would stake out a place in a cramped waiting room overflowing with kids and stage moms. Most times we'd have to wait an hour or more for the actual audition. It was hell.

Mothers would jockey for empty seats in metal folding chairs and chitchat. The fidgety kids were relegated to the floor and ordered to do their homework or doodle on paper. Eventually, some kid would crack, losing his mind from the boredom, and whine like a stuck pig. The casting director would usually appear just in time to see a stressed-out mom twisting "Little Billy's" forearm. That kind of sadistic parenting technique never got good results. Little Billy's whining always got louder, and the casting director would order the kid and mom to go outside to restore order. Of course, that kind of thing never happened to Stan or me. *Not!* I've still got the Indian burn scars on my forearms from my mom's attempts to stop my bitching and moaning.

If you survived the wait in the outer office, and your brain hadn't gone to mush, the casting director would call out your name and lead you to an inner office. Once there, you'd be presented to a parole board of stern-looking adults. These solemn people were the producers and director, the people that do the hiring. They'd study your every move as you read lines like: "I can run really fast in my new Keds sneakers!" or "Ipana toothpaste tastes suuuuuper!"

Once you finished the reading, the director would mumble: "Thanks for coming. Next." The casting director would then give you the *bum's rush* out the door. You were in the inner sanctum for no more than a minute. It seemed like a helluva long trek to *North* Hollywood just for that.

After a few dozen auditions, Stan and I started to get the hang of things and we booked a couple of projects. I got a Buster Brown shoes commercial, and Stan booked a couple of TV shows, *The Whirly Birds* and *The Bonnie Parker Story*. My parents were completely amazed when Stan landed a really plum job in a big MGM movie, *Please Don't Eat the Daisies*. It starred Doris Day! She was one of the biggest stars in the world.

Stan and I suddenly had acting careers, and this really pleased my mom. The success of her children gave her bragging rights. It also gave her a project to pour her pent-up energy into.

My dad was pleased, too, but as usual was pretty negative and pessimistic about our future as actors. I say this about him with no malice whatsoever. I loved my dad. He was a brilliant, gentle soul who rarely lost his temper, unlike my mom who could turn on you like a pit bull. He just couldn't embrace the idea of schlepping his kids all over the city for auditions. It was too much of a distraction from his favorite pastime: analyzing the mysterious demons in his head that were holding him back. Unfortunately, his dark deliberations never yielded any conclusions, just more questions and angst.

Stan's recent film work on TV, coupled with the *Daisies* film, was now making him recognizable, famous even. I was wowed. My brother was a *Movie Star!* I was proud as hell of him, and he was still my hero. Secretly, though, I was a little jealous of the new perks that were coming his way. Sibling rivalry, I suppose.

Young pretty girls at the pool giggled when Stan arrived; the guys chose him first to play Marco Polo; even aunts and uncles fawned all over him during visits. I noticed how fame changes the way people relate to you. Plain and simple, they like you better. Not a bad thing to aspire to when you're five years old. I craved for a piece of that fame pie, too.

I finally got my first major movie acting job in 1958 when I tagged along with my brother who was auditioning for a movie called *Rally 'Round the Flag, Boys!* The film was going to star a hot young actor, Paul Newman, and his wife, Joanne Woodward; Stan was being considered for a role as one of their sons. Right after his audition, he was offered the part. When the producers saw me in the waiting room and found out we were brothers, I was asked to read for the role of the younger son. I got the job on the spot, too. Bingo! The sibling rivalry eased now that the playing field had leveled.

The start of filming was an exciting time. Especially the first day when we drove through the gates of the mighty film factory, 20th Century-Fox. I finally made it inside a "fort," given permission to pass by the uniformed guards. I was working for the company that made stars of Henry Fonda, Tyrone Power, Betty Grable, and the biggest child star of all time, Shirley Temple.

Some actors make their screen debuts in very dramatic ways: John Wayne, Winchester in hand, flagging down help in *Stage Coach*, or Peter O'Toole galloping across the Arabian desert on a camel wearing a flowing white gown and a golden headdress in *Lawrence of Arabia*. My debut in *Rally 'Round the Flag, Boys!* was upside down, being pile driven into the ground like a posthole digger.

When I first appear in the movie, Joanne Woodward is holding me in the air by both feet, talking into a phone cradled against her shoulder and shaking me up and down. I had supposedly swallowed a penny, and she was trying to dislodge the coin from my gullet. We did this scene numerous times. I don't know who suffered more: me, who was hanging upside down, or Woodward, who had to do the heavy lifting. Despite the strain, she was sweet and gentle as a movie mom could be. I had one heckuva headache after we were done filming.

Paul Newman, ever the method actor, tried to foster a fatherly relationship with his "boys," popping into our schoolroom to chat and sometimes help with our work. The only "fly in the ointment" was our director, a cranky old-timer named Leo McCarey, who was known for directing the Marx Brothers classic *Duck Soup*. McCarey had a reputation as a screamer, the kind of set boss who would verbally abuse an actor if they messed up. At first, McCarey seemed to like me and was satisfied with my acting. Then, one day, everything changed.

We were shooting a scene in the family living room. Stan and I were directed to keep our eyes glued on a TV set, engrossed in a program, while Newman entered the front door.

"Ignore him, no matter what he does or says, just keep watching the TV," ordered McCarey. Easy enough, I thought. We did that all the time with our real parents.

Take one: Newman made his entrance and paused behind the sofa where Stan and I were sitting. He says, "Hi, boys!" We give him nothing back, ignoring him. Then he waved, still trying to get our attention, and we stayed riveted to the TV as instructed.

McCarey's voice yells out from behind the camera, "Cut! Let's do it again. Barry, keep your eyes on the TV."

I replied, "Huh? Uh . . . okay."

Take two: Newman enters, tries to get us to look at him. Once again, I am focused on the TV.

"*Cut!*" screamed McCarey. "Barry, you're not looking at the TV like I told you to do. Now let's get it right this time!"

Take three: Newman enters and . . .

"*Cuutt!*" We didn't even get to the part where Newman says *Hi*.

McCarey emerged from the darkness, his eyes bulging, jowls jiggling. He gets right in my face and snarls, "Barry, you keep looking away from the TV! Don't do that! Do you understand? Keep your eyes on the TV! *Please!*" Then he retreated into the darkness behind the camera like a pissed-off ghost.

Take four: McCarey bellows, "*Action!*" . . . "*Cut!*" McCarey reappears again, looking like he wants to slap me silly. By this time I am ready to slap myself silly. I didn't know what I was doing wrong; I had never, before or since, looked at a TV as hard as I was doing it that day.

Before McCarey could throttle my neck, Newman intervened. The star said, "Leo, take it easy, he's just a kid. Listen, I've got an idea: You've already got a master shot where you see me enter and come up behind him, right? All you really need is the boy's close-up to show that's he's watching the TV and ignoring me. Let's just shoot that now and let the kid rest. It'll work out when you edit." The star was already thinking like an award-winning director, which he later became.

Not wanting to waste more time and money, McCarey agreed to Newman's suggestion.

We began my close-ups with high hopes. After one take, it was back to the same old nightmare with McCarey screaming, "Barry, you're still not looking where you should be looking; your eyes are all over the place!"

Newman, ever the hero and cool dude, decided to crawl inside the empty TV cabinet off-camera and give me something interesting to focus on. To make his live presentation more entertaining, a prop master delivered a hand puppet to Newman so he could wave it at me.

While the whole hubbub was unfolding off-camera, I sat there thinking: There is Paul Newman, a major movie star, waving a hand puppet at me from inside an empty television cabinet. Weird.

A couple more aborted takes ensued. Finally, there was an eerie quiet from behind the camera. I heard urgent, unintelligible whispered words offstage and one of them sounded like s*eizure*. I didn't know what the word meant, but it didn't sound good. Then McCarey, Newman, and my studio teacher approached me. The teacher felt my forehead and gently asked, "Barry, are you all right?"

"I feel fine," I replied. And I did, too, except for the embarrassment of Newman's puppet show.

The three adults hovered over me. Their expressions weren't showing frustration anymore, only grave concern. I heard a voice in the darkness behind the camera whisper, "Call an ambulance."

Moments later, my mother and I were being whisked away,

sirens blaring, to the nearest hospital. In the ER, the doctors ruled out seizures as the cause for my wandering eyes. I seemed to be healthy as far as they could tell.

After that, the hospital's ophthalmologist was called in to perform some tests. His diagnosis: astigmatism. That explained why my eyes were randomly darting back and forth, like a broken cuckoo clock. He prescribed glasses to remedy the problem.

After the eye doctor's exam, I was led into another room where a big wooden box was set in front of me. A nurse carefully opened the lid, as if it contained something rare and valuable, like rubies or even kryptonite. Inside the box, on a bed of blue velvet, were . . . eyeglasses. There were round wire-rimmed ones, massive steel rectangles, and stately tortoise shell designs. I was told to pick from the selection. This clearly was an important life decision; a whole new identity would be defined by this choice.

Frankly, I wasn't too pleased about the whole scenario. I didn't really want glasses. They were for the weirdos at school, the oddballs everybody called "four eyes." Then something dawned on me: Superman wore glasses, when he was Clark Kent, anyway. I also remembered seeing Buddy Holly wearing big horn-rimmed spectacles, and the girls still seemed to think he was pretty neat. Even my dad wore glasses, and he was the smartest guy in the world. My anxiety eased.

I reached for the horn-rimmed glasses, put them on, and gazed in the mirror. I liked what I saw. I looked more intelligent than before. I already had a feeling that I was above average in intelligence, but this new prop really sold the idea.

Presto, chango! Just like that, a new me was hatched. I now had horn-rimmed glasses to go along with my large buckteeth and my Moe Howard bowl cut. I believe this new persona was correctly identified decades later and given the proper label: *nerd.* Jim Carrey may have actually borrowed this look for his character in *Dumb and Dumber*. He either took it from me or from Jerry Lewis in *The Nutty Professor*. One way or the other, all

three of us were nerdy dead ringers. I had the dubious distinction of being the first on the block with that particular look.

When I returned to the *Rally 'Round the Flag, Boys!* set the
next day, I was sporting my glasses, and the film's producer
wasn't pleased. Apparently, it was already a stretch in his mind
that Paul Newman's son would have buckteeth and a cheap
bowl haircut. Add on the horn-rimmed glasses, I suddenly looked
like Mr. Moto, the bespectacled Japanese movie spy. That was a
creepy image, far from the ideal 1950s American boy. Actually,
my brother Stan was a great example of that prototype: blond
hair, blue eyes, little freckles on the nose. He was a lovely little
Aryan child, a real purebred. As for me, I was a mutt, lovable but
not yet ready for prime time.

The producers told my mom that I would have to be let go.
They tried to buffer the blow by saying that I could remain
on the production as a "stand-in" for the child actor who was
going to replace me. She rejected their offer and grandly
announced, "My Barry is going to be a star, not a stand-in!"

I'm sure her bold declaration, done in my presence, was
meant to bolster my hurt feelings. After that single outburst, she
clammed up. She couldn't afford to get overly indignant or Stan
might get fired, too. We were just actors, after all, employees like
everybody else. I was politely asked to leave . . . now.

As our car passed through the "fort's" main gates, I grumbled
to my mom, "This is how Johnny Yuma from TV's *The Rebel*
must have felt." It was one of my favorite Westerns, and during
the show's opening credits Johnny was stripped of his soldier's
stripes, tossed out through the gates of Fort Apache, and left to
wander a desert wasteland. I was being ejected, too, for the
unforgivable crime of looking too weird.

Once I was back home, I felt like Cinderella after the ball. The
day before, I was a pampered rising star at 20th Century-Fox;
now I was headed back to Vine Street Elementary and more
"drop and cover" drills. I was certain my fiery demise would be
coming soon. The only one who truly seemed happy about my

return was that goddamn carpenter bee in the telephone pole. On my first walk home after school, he took after me with a vengeance, like he really missed me.

Even though another child actor replaced me in *Rally 'Round the Flag, Boys!* I still consider this my film debut. That's because I'm still in it. Remember the scene where Woodward was holding me in the air by my shoes and tapping my head on the floor? The producers decided to use it. I was upside down anyway and practically unrecognizable. For the following scenes in the movie, when the son is upright, it is the kid who replaced me. The producers figured nobody would notice. And nobody did . . . except me.

CHAPTER 4

A Well-Rounded Performer

 After being fired on my first movie, my mom began hustling me around the town for more auditions. Nothing much came my way, though. I had hit a lull. Our agent put it in my mom's head that Stan and I needed to cultivate more skills in the performing arts if we were to increase our odds at booking jobs. I started hearing the phrase "well-rounded performer" a lot.

"The people who make it in show business aren't just merely actors; they also dance, sing, and play musical instruments like Gene Kelly or Fred Astaire. Those guys are really *well-rounded* performers!" my mom would exclaim.

This was an era when tap dancing was still thought to be the height of artistic expression . . . along with playing an accordion. If you could do both, the next stop was *The Ed Sullivan Show.*

Stan and I were soon enrolled in Madame Etienne's Dance Academy on Hollywood Boulevard. We joined a chorus line of aspiring child stars, learning our tap "time steps," sashaying to rumbas and slinking across the academy's glossy hardwood floors with some pretty sexy jazz moves. When I saw myself gyrating in the floor-to-ceiling mirror, I definitely didn't see suave Gene Kelly looking back. With my big glasses and buckteeth, I looked like Theodore from *Alvin and the Chipmunks*, and he sure as hell was a crappy dancer.

Stan and I sacrificed our Saturday morning cartoons every weekend for the next year to attend the academy. I worked hard to learn jazz, ballet, and tap. You had to. If you lagged behind, Madame Etienne would whack you on the butt with her cane. Long ago, perhaps the turn of the twentieth century, she danced with the Moscow Ballet Company. She was a diva from a foreign land and took no guff.

After dance class, my mom shuttled me to a different school to learn another kind of performing art: ice-skating. That was fun. Our classes were held at the Polar Palace, which burned down in the 1960s. (How an ice rink could catch fire was beyond me.) The Polar Palace held a huge oval ice arena that was as big as a football field. I learned to twirl, do a single-axel jump, and skate backward. According to my mother, you never knew when a job call might come along looking for the next Dick Button.

Now that I was on the road to becoming a well-rounded performer, I started to book more jobs. That was my mom's rationale, anyway, which I realized was a clever ruse to keep me going to dance classes. I knew that my clumsy modern jazz skills had nothing to do with getting hired for a 1963 Western, *The Travels of Jaimie McPheeters*, starring a young Kurt Russell. I wasn't required to flamenco dance on *The Dick Powell Theatre*, either. Moms just can't be trusted sometimes.

The latter program was a dramatic anthology, and the episode I did was called "Somebody Is Waiting," starring Mickey Rooney. He was one of the biggest child stars ever, a top box-office draw in the 1940s, and had become an acclaimed adult performer. In fact, he won an Emmy for his performance in this drama playing a lonely merchant marine sailor who is killed while on shore leave.

The director thought he'd be clever and get my "real" reaction to Mickey's death scene. I heard him whisper to the cameraman, "roll film," and then he told me to ride my bike down a studio alley where I found Rooney lying on the ground, blood oozing from his mouth.

Rooney gasped, "Little boy, help me . . . help me!" I was a seasoned pro by now and instantly knew they were trying to trick me. I played along anyway. I gave out a yelp and a shudder, the one that I'd practiced the night before while learning my scene with my dad. The director loved it, assuming he outsmarted me. I just accepted the compliments, never mentioning that I was onto their scheme.

CHAPTER 5

Working with Legends

 My brother started a new acting job that would eventually play a major role in my budding career, too. Stan became a recurring character on *The Adventures of Ozzie and Harriet* playing a neighbor boy, Stanley.

The long-running series was in its latter years and Ozzie's real-life sons, Rick and David (characters on the show), were too old to hang out with their Pop all the time. Ozzie cast Stan to inject a little youthful energy into his show, somebody he could pal around with and go to the malt shop with, without looking like a pedophile. The show epitomized a 1950s *Pleasantville* reality. Ozzie never went to work and always had tons of free time to goof off. Nice life, if you can get it.

Ozzie's character was famous for his stuttering, stammering speech pattern. That wasn't by choice. He spoke that way because he didn't have time to remember his lines. He was too busy writing, directing, and producing practically every episode during the show's sixteen-year run. When it came time to film his scenes, he'd read his lines off a teleprompter and fumble his way through the action with the other actors. The result was a lovable, bumbling, befuddled TV dad. In reality, though, he was a creative dynamo, perhaps television's first *auteur*.

On the days that my brother worked on *Ozzie and Harriet*, my mom would haul me down to the set, too. It wasn't because we couldn't afford a babysitter; my mother wanted to let Ozzie know that I was available, too. Sure enough, her crafty little plan worked. Eventually, Ozzie asked if I would like to do an episode. She was always thinking ahead.

Ozzie wanted to use me in a school classroom scene. I was supposed to stand at a blackboard and write out a complicated math problem, much to his character's befuddlement. I reported to the studio on my designated day of filming and, to my surprise, another crisis unfolded.

It turned out that I was too short to do the scene. I couldn't reach high enough on the blackboard to write out the math formula so the camera could see it over the heads of the students. If the camera can't see it, you're screwed. Ozzie pondered the dilemma and decided that he had no choice but to go with the quickest, easiest solution: get a taller kid.

Holy crap. I couldn't believe it. I was getting canned again. The last time I was too weird looking; this time I was too damn small. It felt like there was an insidious plan afoot to destroy my morale and dignity. Thank God, Ozzie was no maniacal screamer like the first director who fired me. He assured me that I'd get another role soon. True to his word, Ozzie hired me a few weeks later.

On my next episode, we were shooting a scene in the Nelsons' TV kitchen, where there were no height requirements. I was asked to do something that I was very capable of: eat chocolate ice cream. In fact, I got so absorbed in my delicious task that I forgot to say my lines in the first take. Ozzie understood kids, though, and was amused by my mistake. He gently reminded me that I should eat my ice cream *and* say my lines. If I did a good job, I could have all the ice cream I wanted. Now that's the kind of director I liked working with.

When the episode finally aired, my performance was pretty amusing. I had chocolate ice cream smeared all around my mouth. Whenever I had a line of dialogue, I'd barely lift my face out of the bowl to speak. The second I finished talking, I dove back into the scrumptious dessert. The scene was funny because it was honest, exactly the kind of behavior a real kid would do in such a moment. Ozzie was a master at recognizing those "little truths" and using them. I just wanted to eat as much ice cream as I could.

I became a member of Ozzie Nelson's repertory of recurring characters, and I was treated like family. Whenever I worked on the show, Ozzie invited me to have lunch with him in his personal screening room. We would watch the "dailies" (rough footage of scenes shot the day before). After finishing our main courses, an assistant would deliver our favorite dessert: chocolate ice cream. I think he liked the stuff as much as I did.

Ozzie was my first acting teacher, too. He imparted two basic and important lessons: Number one, *relax*. Relaxation is key to every good performance. Lesson number two: Look at the other actors when they're talking, listen to what they're saying, and when it's your turn to speak, answer them with your scripted lines. It is simple advice but profoundly true to the art of fine acting. Ask any good actor and they'll agree.

Now that I was appearing regularly on the Nelsons' hit show, my agent started receiving requests for my services. That was a big step up from the "cattle call" auditions. I became a known commodity, a "Barry Livingston type," which amazed everyone in our family.

A couple of interesting roles were offered to me that involved working with two comedy icons. The first job was with that other seminal nerd, Jerry Lewis, who was a god to most kids of my age. I was the envy of all my young pals when I told them that I was going to be in his next film, *The Errand Boy.*

In the movie, Lewis plays a lowly movie studio employee, an errand boy. My character, a child actor, comes into the studio's candy store where Lewis is working. I repeatedly ask him to fetch different-colored jelly beans from jars high atop some shelves. Lewis is forced to climb the store's tall, rolling ladder so many times that he snaps. His broad reaction, a frustration that slowly builds to an explosion, is hysterical. It's a classic routine that has become known as the "Jelly Bean" scene to many of his fans. I'm honored to have been a small part of it.

Lewis wrote and directed the movie as well as starred in it, so I got to watch him work in multiple roles. He displayed more nervous energy than most hyperactive kids at my elementary school. One day, Lewis was so manic and out of control that he darted in front of a moving camera dolly and got clobbered. The dolly hit him so hard in the head that it drew blood and knocked him right on his ass.

After working with Lewis, I was cast in a small part in a movie with another comedy giant, my *Honeymooners* hero, Jackie Gleason. The film was *Papa's Delicate Condition*, and the "Great One" was larger than life. Nothing seemed to rattle his jovial mood, not even smashing his "Rolls Royce" golf cart into the back of somebody's shiny new Cadillac. Gleason was another comedy giant with a thirst for life . . . and alcohol.

CHAPTER 6

Memories Are Magic

The Dick Van Dyke Show was my first acting job where I performed in front of a live audience, which I assumed would be easy. I was pretty cocky for a nine-year-old thespian, having already logged five years in the "biz." That was halfway to qualifying for my Screen Actor's Guild pension, which meant I could retire at fourteen! I had things all figured out. Or so I thought.

My role in the episode wasn't that complicated. I played a friend of Richie Petrie (Van Dyke's TV son). The boy boasted that his dad owned the wildest pair of pajamas ever made. I doubted him, and so Richie takes me to view the amazing pj's while his father is in bed sleeping. Carl Reiner, the show's creator, gave me one specific direction: go slack-jawed in shock when the pajamas are revealed. Easy enough. It was money in the bank.

We rehearsed the show for four days. Reiner staged our action, jokes were honed, and my "slack-jawed" reaction met with everybody's approval. One element missing in rehearsals, though: Van Dyke's spectacular pajamas. Either the star didn't feel like wearing them or there was a calculated plan to reveal the pj's on filming day, hoping to catch my "real" reaction. I suspected it was the latter, mainly because I overheard Reiner tell Van Dyke that the audience will howl when they see the goofy kid's stunned expression. *Goofy kid?* I thought I looked like Steve McQueen. Another illusion shattered.

On the fifth day of work we were ready to film the show. A chattering crowd streamed into the studio, filling the air with electricity, and that triggered a sensation that I'd never felt before: preshow *butterflies.* The mere thought of people watching me onstage caused a tingling from my groin to my stomach. That's when I started to worry. I'd heard disaster stories about other actors whose jitters grew into full-blown stage fright. Sometimes they'd go into total paralysis or break into tears and run offstage. *That couldn't happen to me,* I reassured myself. *I was a pro, ready for anything!*

Suddenly, a loud bell rang on the stage, filming had commenced, and the *flitting butterflies* morphed into *flapping crows.* I wasn't ready for that. The hands on a wall clock backstage seemed to be spinning faster and faster, hurtling me toward my moment of truth. Before you could scream *run,* I heard my cue to enter the scene . . . and I did.

I followed Richie through the Petries' TV living room (being careful not to do a pratfall over Van Dyke's famous ottoman). Perspiration beaded on my forehead, and it wasn't from the hot studio lights. I felt the "multiheaded monster" in the studio bleachers watching us, daring me to look at them, but I resisted . . . and continued to sweat.

Richie and I crept into a bedroom where we found Rob Petrie (Van Dyke) "sleeping" in his bed. A blanket covered his body and, of course, the awesome pajamas.

Richie held an index finger to his lips and peeled back the covers. Ever so slowly, the pajamas were revealed. It was a two-piece suit, bright orange with black stripes. Van Dyke's head looked like it was attached to the body of a Bengal tiger.

The audience roared with laughter, and their energy surged over me; that was another odd, new feeling. A nervous giggle started to work its way up from my gut to my "frozen, slack-jawed mouth." Suddenly, I began laughing! Of course, that was not part of the plan.

An unseen voice, like a displeased god, boomed through overhead speakers: "Cut!" A stage bell rang twice, which meant that filming was aborted. Suddenly, things weren't so funny.

Van Dyke opened his eyes, looked at me, and frowned. Even more troubling, Carl Reiner, the show's eight-hundred-pound gorilla, walked out from the darkness behind the cameras. He looked disappointed; like I'd spoiled a surprise party that he'd been planning all week.

"You weren't supposed to laugh," he said.

"I'm sorry. I know. I couldn't help . . ."

Reiner interrupted me and said, "Let's try it again. When you see Richie's dad, just drop your jaw and stare. Nothing more."

"Okay," I replied firmly, trying to regain his confidence, and mine, too.

Take two: Richie and I sneak into the bedroom, my pal pulls down the covers revealing the Van Dyke–Bengal tiger, the audience laughs, and . . . I follow their lead, turning into Chuckles the Chimp, again.

"Cut!" The stage bell banged loudly, signaling the end of filming, and perhaps my career.

Goddamn that audience, I hissed to myself while still giggling. I'd lost all self-control.

Reiner was on the set within seconds this time. His disappointment now looked like frustration.

"What happened?" he snapped.

"I . . . uh . . . I laughed 'cause the audience . . ."

"The audience can laugh, not you. It kills 'the funny' if you think it's funny," said the wise man of comedy. "Understand?"

I nodded *uh-huh* but I didn't really understand. I figured I better pretend or get fired on the spot.

Reiner was no rube, though, and saw that I was scared and bluffing. He knelt down, gently patted my cheek, and whispered:

"Think about something you remember, something that shocked you. Memories are like magic, you know. Just relax and go with it. Okay?"

I nodded *yes*, but I still didn't really know what he meant. *Memories? Magic?* The "old pro" was clueless but game.

Take three: Richie and I enter, the pj's are revealed, my jaw sagged, the audience screamed, and just as I feared, another tickle started to percolate in my innards.

What the hell is wrong with me? I've never had this problem before! my brain screamed. The giggle kept rising. If it reached my mouth, I was screwed, the jig up, my acting reputation toast.

Then a miracle happened. The memory of my dog, Lady, popped into my mind's eye, and it wasn't a pretty picture. *My pet was lying in the street after a car had run her over; she was dead.* Granted, the image wasn't the same kind of shock as seeing somebody's dad in funny pajamas, but I was grateful that something, *anything*, popped into my head. I decided to go with the memory as Reiner suggested and focused on *Lady's black eyes, glassy and motionless, and her furry midsection that looked flattened by the tire that rolled over her.* Not surprisingly, the tickle began to recede.

The audience was not to be spurned, though. They howled like Greek sirens luring me onto the rocks. I fought back with another memory: a *grumpy city worker scooping up my dead pet with a big shovel and flinging her limp body into the back of his truck.* Believe me, my "stunned, frozen slack jaw" has never hung lower.

At last, the scene ended. The studio bell dinged, just like it does at the end of a boxing match; I had finally won the bout.

Reiner returned to the set and pronounced me a comedy genius. Well, not actually. He just thanked me, I assumed for not screwing up his show, again, and the cast and crew moved on to the next scene. My work was done, not a moment too soon, and I was sent packing.

Driving home from the studio, my mom could see me lost in

thought. "Don't worry, Barry," she said. "People make mistakes. There's a lot to learn."

"Uh-huh," I mumbled. I hated when adults said things like that. Secretly, I was still rattled but couldn't admit it. My first live performance was a disaster, and that took my cockiness down a couple of notches. Perhaps I didn't have it all figured out.

We rode in silence, and then my mother asked, "So, what did Mr. Reiner finally tell you?"

I sighed, wanting to put the whole weird evening behind me, and said, "I forget." Of course, that wasn't true because the director's words were still echoing in my head. So was my dog's ghostly memory. Lady's appearance was a godsend and a revelation. She was still alive, somewhere in my body or soul, and I had the power to call upon her. My dog could still come to my rescue if I ever needed her help.

Reiner was right. Memories are like magic.

CHAPTER 7

The Top Secret TV Series

 While I was busy working in movies, Stan was on the verge of an acting break that would change his life forever, and eventually mine, too.

Our agent told Stan that he had an audition for an untitled, top-secret project. Our family was intrigued. Nothing grabs your attention more than a super-classified project. The only thing that could be revealed: a huge movie star was attached to the enterprise, which was a pilot for a new TV series. This was an era when major film stars rarely appeared in TV projects; it was considered beneath their stature. This series was going to be very special.

At Stan's audition, he learned that the untitled project actually had a name: *My Three Sons.* Somebody also leaked the name of the show's star: Fred MacMurray. MacMurray was a *huge* movie star, having come off a string of Disney hits like *The Absent-Minded Professor* and *The Shaggy Dog.* Preceding those movies, MacMurray's film career went back another thirty years and included such classics as *Double Indemnity, The Egg and I,* and *The Caine Mutiny.* How was a star of MacMurray's stature lured to TV? There was one overriding factor.

MacMurray wanted a change in lifestyle. Movie work often required him to leave home and travel abroad or labor at the studio for long hours, putting in twelve- to fifteen-hour days.

MacMurray wanted out of that madness because he and his wife, June Haver, had recently adopted twin girls. He dreamed of a job that would give him regular workdays with set hours. Plain and simple: MacMurray wanted to be a father more than he needed to be a movie star.

The creator of *My Three Sons,* Don Fedderson, knew of Mac-Murray's desire and made him an offer he couldn't refuse. The deal specified that MacMurray would work only two months per season. There'd be no late nights on the set, either. He'd start at 8 a.m. and punch out at 5 p.m. Overtime would cost the company a pretty penny.

A novel way of shooting was devised to accommodate the star's schedule. It became known throughout the industry as the MacMurray Method. In the two months that he was present, the film company would shoot *only* his scenes and *only* his close-ups, sometimes working out of ten different scripts a day to capture his footage from every episode. Once he was gone, the other series regulars would continue shooting the scenes that the star wasn't in and doing their close-ups with a script girl who was reading MacMurray's lines off-camera. It was a wildly unorthodox way of shooting a television series and a production nightmare. Normally, each episode is started and completed in about a week. If you have clout, though, the rules will change. MacMurray definitely had clout. It was an opportunity too good for him to pass up.

After one audition, the producers told Stan that he got the job of Chip Douglas, the youngest of the sons. Stan was the first series regular hired after MacMurray, so our family became privy to the machinations behind some of the early casting decisions.

William Frawley, best known as Fred Mertz from the TV classic *I Love Lucy,* came on board to portray Uncle Bub, the show's nanny. Bobby Diamond, from the TV Western *Fury,* was offered the role of oldest son but couldn't come to terms in negotiations. He was out. MacMurray suggested Tim Considine for the role since they had just worked together on a Disney film,

The Shaggy Dog. When the boss suggests things, people listen. Considine was hired as the oldest son, Mike. To complete the troika of *My Three Sons*, Ryan O'Neal was cast as Robbie, the middle son.

Soon after work on the pilot began, things went sour and filming was halted. MacMurray felt that O'Neal wasn't up to par with his comedy skills (he proved everybody wrong later in his career) and was let go. A mad search went out to replace him. My mother mentioned the talent hunt to Mary Grady, an agent specializing in child actors. She happened to be the mother of Don Grady, who was already famous as a Mousketeer on the *Mickey Mouse Club.* Mary got her son an audition, and Don won the part of Robbie, the middle son. The original cast of *MTS* was solidified.

In 1960, the concept for *MTS* was quite fresh and new: a widowed father struggling to raise his three boys in an all-male household. It was a radical departure from the other TV family shows that were popular at the time such as *The Donna Reed Show, Ozzie and Harriet,* and *Father Knows Best.* Those shows had two loving parents raising their children in spotless households in near perfect harmony. *MTS* was going to depict a new kind of American family: a single parent with kids. This prototype was to become a staple in films and on TV shows years later.

Don Fedderson is cited as the "creator" of *MTS,* but Peter Tewksbury, the pilot's director, was a major force in developing the show's originality. He fleshed out the brotherly relationships and shaped the whimsical comedic tone that became a hallmark of the show.

Tewksbury decided that the all-male household of *MTS,* lacking the feminine touch, would be in a constant state of disarray with the family dog asleep on the recliner, crumpled laundry piling up on the sofa, and stacks of mealtime dishes in the sink. Tewksbury also told the younger sons, Chip and Robbie, to take a shortcut midway down the staircase and leap over the banister. These were hardly revolutionary ideas, but they were true to the show's premise and created a new, perhaps more honest, version of an American household.

When the pilot aired in 1960, the viewing audience saw a lot of themselves in this new TV family and fell in love. Every girl wanted to coddle this motherless clan, and every boy wanted to join their chaotic ranks. The show was an instant smash hit.

Thirty-nine episodes were filmed in the first season. Working in multiple episodes every day was key to making the MacMurray Method viable. Every day there was a frantic daily scramble to film the star's scenes. Occasionally, only half a scene would be filmed, if MacMurray's character exited in the middle of the action. In such cases, the actors would freeze in place the second he walked off camera and a still photographer would take a Polaroid picture catching the moment.

Months later, when it was time to complete the scene, the actors would look at the Polaroid photo, assume the "frozen" positions, and then pick up the action from there. Once the editors assembled all the footage, the final cut would look seamless, like it was all shot on the same day.

Maintaining continuity was the biggest challenge to success of the MacMurray Method. Hair would have to be kept at the same length and color all season long; an actor's weight couldn't fluctuate, either. Occasionally, Mother Nature had her say because the younger sons, Stan and Don, were still growing. A sudden growth spurt could easily occur in the intervening months between filming parts of the same scene. Wardrobe that fit in January might be too small in June. To deal with such problems, the costume designer bought doubles of everything: shirts, pants, dress suits. Sometimes he'd even buy larger sizes of the same outfits, trying to outwit Mother Nature's whims.

Credit should be given where credit is due. The production manager for *MTS*, John Stephens, was the scheduling wizard who made sure that no shot was forgotten. Without Stephens keeping track of every missing scene, half-scene, or matching close-up, the MacMurray Method would have collapsed into

MacMurray Madness. The star realized his importance to the show, too.

Stephens had a salary dispute with Don Fedderson one year, and the boss told him that he was fired. Before walking off the studio lot, Stephens stopped by MacMurray's trailer to say good-bye. Once the star heard about Stephens's leaving, he immediately got on the phone to Fedderson. Stephens was rehired that same day, with a substantial raise. Money was never better spent.

CHAPTER 8

Moving Up in the World

Now that my brother was working full-time on *MTS*, Ozzie Nelson needed someone to fill Stan's recurring role on his show. He didn't have to look far. Since I'd already done a couple of episodes, Ozzie was familiar with my acting ability, and our mutual love of chocolate ice cream. I officially became Barry, the little neighbor boy, who would accompany Oz to the malt shop or play catch with him.

My stature as a child actor took a big leap when the Nelsons gave me my first "guest star billing." It was in an episode that Ozzie specifically wrote for me called "The Little House Guest."

The story called for my character to spend the night with the Nelsons. My parents were going to the hospital to have a baby, and I was dead set on having a little brother. Ozzie, Harriet, Rick, and Dave had to convince me that a baby sister would be just as good as a baby brother, but my preference in genders was unwavering. In the end, after a few trips to the malt shop and a couple of bowls of chocolate ice cream, Ozzie's gentle counseling won me over.

There was one other very cool perk that I got while working with the Nelsons: watching Rick Nelson, a major rock-and-roll star, premiere new songs like "Hello, Mary Lou" or "Travelin' Man" on the show. Ozzie was no dummy. He understood the power of the TV medium in selling a product. Whenever Rick was about to release his next single, Ozzie wrote a high school sock-hop scene into an episode so his son could perform the song. A TV audience of thirty million people would hear it, and the record would zoom to number one across the country. It was MTV the Ozzie Nelson way.

Suddenly, I was earning good money with the Nelsons and Stan was pulling down a big weekly paycheck as a series regular on *MTS*. By law, parents of working children are entitled to a portion of their kids' earnings but only after a percentage of their salary is set aside and put into a trust account. The child actors can collect the trust money when they turn eighteen. This regulation is known as the Coogan Law, enacted after an early child star, Jackie Coogan, saw his entire fortune squandered by his reckless parents.

My parents generously decided to exceed the minimum requirement of 10 percent set aside in a trust and raised it to 20 percent. The parents could use the remaining 80 percent in any way they deemed necessary. This was fine by my brother and me, especially since our standard of living was on the rise. Not long before the showbiz bucks starting rolling in, we were near the poverty level. Now we were on the fast track toward a respectable middle-class lifestyle.

One of the family's first luxury purchases was a two-door, canary yellow Cadillac, a beautiful tank. My most vivid memory of the Caddie is how heavy it seemed, particularly the doors after my mom accidentally slammed my hand in one. Fortunately, I was such a little guy that my mitt was only squished and not broken.

My parents also bought a house in Laurel Canyon in the Hollywood Hills. The rough-and-tumble street scene on Wilcox Avenue was replaced by the serene beauty of the canyon.

I enrolled in a new school, too, Wonderland Avenue Elementary. Making new friends was especially hard in the Canyon because everybody lived so far apart; houses were spread out all over the mountain. At my old apartment, I had a slew of pals living right next door. My new home was like an outpost on the moon.

Needless to say, I wasn't happy until I made a startling discovery. The sprawling property next door to us once belonged to the infamous magician Harry Houdini. His ghost supposedly haunted a burned-down mansion there. Laurel Canyon suddenly got a whole lot more interesting.

Harry Houdini died years earlier, and his abandoned property had become a jungle of plants and shrubs. The ruins of his stately home had been swallowed up by the foliage like some buried Mayan temple. It was creepy as hell. According to legend, Houdini regularly held séances and was able to contact the dead. Some of my new classmates swore that a ghost walked the property every full moon . . . armed with an axe. Some even said that Houdini actually died on the property after somebody lodged the same axe in his back. An axe is always a swell schoolyard embellishment. It didn't take much to convince me that every gruesome tale was true; my imagination was scarred by too many gory Roger Corman monster movies.

As the next full moon approached, a debate raged between my brother and me: should we face our fears and explore the foreboding grounds or was it just too dangerous to mess with Houdini's ghost? I argued for the latter . . . and lost. Younger brothers usually do in such matters. A nighttime excursion was planned with a few old pals from Wilcox Street.

The night of the full moon arrived. Stan, Ray Canada, Alan Nickolleti, and I hiked up into the hills and entered the estate from the rear by climbing a rotted wooden fence. My heart pounded so hard I could hear it. If the ghost wasn't scary enough, we'd recently learned that a surly caretaker also lived somewhere on the property. He was supposedly meaner than hell, no doubt pissed off by the intrusions of kids like us. I knew from experience that angry security guards were just as scary as evil spirits. My eyes were open wide for either man or apparition.

We crept deeper onto the property, picking our way through

a dense jungle, and stumbled upon a stone path. We followed the man-made trail as it snaked through the canopy of towering date palms. It led us straight to the charred ruins of the main house.

There was nothing left of the mansion except for a huge rectangular cement foundation and two stone fireplaces that loomed in the darkness like sentinels. Under the gray moonlight, we scoured the cracked concrete in search of underground secret passages, the main goal of our expedition that night. Had we found one, it would have been like discovering King Tut's tomb; the bragging rights would have lasted a lifetime.

We probed the ground, prying up broken chunks of concrete, and found nothing but dirt. Then, we heard something: a far-off, blood-curdling howl. My body froze and my eyes darted back and forth, trying to penetrate the dark jungle surrounding us. The high-pitched howls grew angrier, more intense. Some kind of monster, alive or dead, was clawing its way through the bushes and closing in on us.

"Let's get out of here!" Stan screamed. I needed no more prompting.

We dove into the thick shrubs. As I ran, tree branches lashed my face, unleashed by the fleeing kid in front of me. Nothing slowed me down, though. I was at the rear of the pack and knew I would be the first to be eaten. Looking over my shoulder, I finally saw a predator tearing through the bushes. It was a sinewy Doberman pinscher in full gallop, twenty yards behind and closing fast.

Up ahead was a chain-link fence. Ray and Alan climbed it in two seconds flat. Just as Stan was about to climb, he looked at me and saw that I wasn't going to escape the canine. Casting his own safety aside, Stan ran back for me like John Wayne returning for a fallen comrade. He grabbed my collar and dragged me to the fence as the Doberman arrived. The mad dog had his pick of legs hanging down and chose Stan's. I only knew this after I heard my brother's panicked cries; I continued to climb the chain link like a scared monkey. It was "fight or flight," and I opted for the latter.

I reached the top of the fence and looked down. It was a terrible sight. The beast's head was flailing back and forth with Stan's leg in its jaws. It looked like a velociraptor toying with a natural enemy before tearing it to pieces. Amid Stan's screams and the dog's guttural snarls, the bottom half of my brother's jeans ripped right off. He was suddenly free of the dog's bite and flew over the fence like a ninja.

We dropped to the ground on the safe side of the fence and watched the insane Doberman gnaw on the fence, trying to chew through steel to get at us. A flashlight's beam sliced through the jungle and was coming our way. I didn't care if it was the caretaker or the ghost of Houdini; I'd had enough fun for one night. I ran home and never looked back.

We lived next to Houdini's mansion for more than three years, and I never ventured back onto the grounds again. In my mind, the Doberman might have been the spirit of the great Houdini himself, and I wasn't taking any chances.

CHAPTER 9

My Six Loves

 I had done two movies for Paramount: *The Errand Boy* and *Papa's Delicate Condition*. I must have impressed somebody at the studio because in late 1962 they offered me a great supporting role in *My Six Loves,* an upcoming film starring Debbie Reynolds and Cliff Robertson.

There were a couple of odd coincidences regarding this project. First, the title of this movie, *My Six Loves,* was similar to my brother's show, *My Three Sons.* Second, between shooting seasons on *MTS,* Stan got a job in an epic Western *How the West Was Won,* which also starred Debbie Reynolds. She was the biggest female star in Hollywood, very much in demand, and worked with me on the weekdays and then flew off to Arizona on the weekends to work with Stan on the Western. This is how Ms. Reynolds came by her reputation as a workaholic.

My Six Loves had another unique distinction. The famed cult novelist, John Fante, author of *Ask the Dust,* wrote the screenplay. Fante was moonlighting to earn some studio bucks to fund his true passion, noir novels about the low life of Los Angeles.

This is only one of two films helmed by the great stage director Gower Champion. He was the guiding force on Broadway behind *Hello Dolly, Bye Bye Birdie,* and *Carnival. My Six Loves* was going to be his big break into films.

Champion liked me and kept adding little moments in scenes

for my character. One unique bit of business was flushing toilets. I played Sherman, one of six hillbilly orphans given refuge by Reynolds at her lavish country home. Champion figured that my character would never have seen indoor plumbing, hence the flushing fixation. The sound of a flushing toilet preceded my entrance into almost every scene, and the gag got quite a laugh in the movie theaters.

Another star in the movie, David Janssen, also took a shine to me. He played a slick showbiz manager and was forever offering me his cigar to smoke in our scenes.

During filming, Debbie Reynolds took my mother aside and said, "Barry has natural comedic timing." That was a great compliment from a hugely talented star, something I'll always cherish.

CHAPTER 10

The Amazing TV

 Whenever I had free time while working on *My Six Loves* at Paramount, I'd explore the lot. You never knew what you'd encounter: Nazi tanks, alien spaceships, movie stars, you name it. One day I spotted a brand-new, gleaming white Cadillac limo that was as long as an oil tanker. It was idling outside a soundstage and the back doors were open. I couldn't resist peeking inside.

The limo's interior was like a vision of heaven, all snowy white and pristine. The ivory-colored carpet was plush as polar bear fur, and the creamy leather seats looked edible, like tuck-and-roll white fudge. A highly polished wooden control board was imbedded in the compartment's ceiling with gold-plated toggle switches. Then, I spotted the most amazing sight of all: a television set! I'd only heard rumors of such advanced technology, and now here it was, man's next great step into the future: mobile entertainment! You could ride all over town, in the lap of limo luxury, and not miss a single second of the best shows: *The Mickey Mouse Club*, *Bugs Bunny*, and *Rin-Tin-Tin*. This idea boggled my eight-year-old mind, particularly since our boxy old Philco TV at home barely got reception unless you slapped the damn thing silly and tweaked its rabbit-ear antennae.

I ogled the limo's television and figured its picture clarity had to be top of the line, just like whoever owned this limo. He was probably a famous inventor like Thomas Edison, or maybe even an astronaut, John Glenn perhaps. Just then, a voice drawled in a deep Southern accent, "Ya like it?"

I turned around to see who could ask such a silly and obvious question. Holy crap! It was Elvis Presley, The King of Rock and Roll. He was towering over me, dressed in a colorful, loose-fitting Hawaiian shirt. His famous upper lip was raised on the left side with a half smile, half sneer, like in pictures I'd seen of him.

"They just finished the custom work and brought it over," Elvis said, stroking the glossy white paint on the car's roof. He leaned over and peered inside the rear compartment. The King's nose was inches away from mine; a loose strand of his raven black hair, slick and shiny, dangled in front of his eyes. "What do ya think?"

Up close, his skin looked smooth as butter because it was coated with a heavy bronze makeup. He almost looked fake, like a walking-talking wax replica of himself. "I like the TV . . .uh . . . Elvis." I said his name tentatively, testing it out to see how he'd react.

He laughed, climbed into the rear cabin, and settled into the leather seat, pushing down on it with his hands, assessing the firmness. Elvis seemed impressed. "I like TV, too," he said. "Let's see what's on."

He flipped one of the gold-plated toggle switches on the overhead console. The television came alive, making an odd sizzling noise, and then a scrambled black-and-white image on the screen became perfectly clear. *I knew it! The picture was better than our crummy old Philco.* Not only that, *Popeye the Sailor*, one of my favorite cartoons, was showing.

"I'm gonna take her for a lil' test drive 'round the lot. Wanna come along?" Elvis asked.

Hell, yeah, I wanted to go! Just then, my mother's stern voice popped into my head: *Never ride with a stranger, Barry.* Then, a different, sneakier voice whispered: *Elvis is no stranger. Every-*

body knows Elvis! He's probably the most famous guy in the world!

"Ya comin'?" Elvis asked again, snapping me out of my reverie.

I glanced up and down the studio's bustling corridor. Mom was nowhere in sight. The temptation was immense. A ride with Elvis was definitely a draw, but the chance to watch Popeye from the back of a rolling limo was the clincher. I hopped in.

Seconds later, Elvis and I were cruising the lot as the limo driver kept the car moving forward at a steady five miles per hour. We sat next to each other, transfixed by the action on TV: *Brutus molested Popeye's girlfriend, Olive Oil, until the scrappy sailor, pumped up on spinach, whomped the bad guy's ass. Popeye's spinning, muscle-swollen forearm socked Brutus so hard that the bearded villain flew into space, orbited the moon twice, and then returned to Earth, landing in a pile of cow crap in a pasture.* Elvis chuckled.

When Popeye began to warble, "I'm Popeye the sailor man," the singer flicked off the set. I figured the sailor's scratchy voice probably bugged Elvis, him being the King and all. Secretly, I was a bit irked. I wanted to watch the cartoon until the very last credit rolled. It was his limo, though, so I didn't whine like I would have if my mom had done such a thing.

Elvis stared out the limo's window and quietly said, "What are ya workin' on?"

"*My Six Loves* . . . with Debbie Reynolds. What are you doing here?"

"*Fun in Acapulco*. It's not as fun as it sounds," he replied with a sigh. He continued to stare out the window in silence. I was hoping he'd turn the TV back on, but he didn't.

We continued our slow-speed tour of the Paramount lot, Elvis staring out the window, me staring at the TV's blank screen.

Eventually, we arrived back at the soundstage, and the limo came to a stop where my amazing journey began.

The limo driver hopped out of his front seat and raced to the rear door, but Elvis had already opened it. The driver, now chagrined and tense, snapped to attention and waited for the King's next move. "Gotta get back to work," said Elvis.

"Me, too . . . I guess," I said.

Elvis climbed out of the car, but I lingered in my seat, taking one last look at mobile television. I wanted to be able to describe it in complete detail to all my doubting friends. They could be pretty hard to sway when it came to futuristic inventions, especially electronic devices that worked without being plugged into a wall outlet.

Elvis, now outside the limo, peered back inside the rear compartment where I was still sitting. That sly, crooked grin formed on his lips, and he said, "*Bugs Bunny* comes on after *Popeye*. If you wanna stay and watch it, you can."

My mouth dropped, surprised by his generous offer. "I wish I could . . . but I'd better get back to my soundstage before my mom worries."

Elvis nodded and said, "See ya, son." He hurried to a nearby stage door, went inside, and didn't look back, which I was hoping he might do. Now that Elvis was gone, the limo driver gave me the ol' stink eye that said, *Beat it, kid, you're trespassing!*

I slowly climbed out of the limo, scanning the area to make sure my mom didn't see me. There'd be hell to pay, Elvis or no Elvis. Luckily, the coast was clear.

I arrived back at my soundstage door and took one last look at the limo. A thought dawned on me that made me smile: Elvis knew when *Bugs Bunny* was coming on. He knew the cartoon schedule!

Long live the King.

CHAPTER 11

My Three Sons

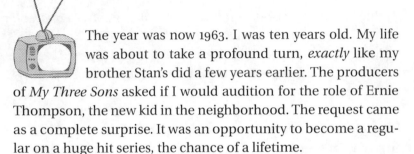 The year was now 1963. I was ten years old. My life was about to take a profound turn, *exactly* like my brother Stan's did a few years earlier. The producers of *My Three Sons* asked if I would audition for the role of Ernie Thompson, the new kid in the neighborhood. The request came as a complete surprise. It was an opportunity to become a regular on a huge hit series, the chance of a lifetime.

I reported to the offices of Don Fedderson, the show's executive producer, and saw that no other child actors were waiting to read. That was surprising. The usual suspects, Bill Mumy, Mark Hamill, or Ron Howard, always seemed to be at the important auditions. This time, though, I was there alone. We figured Fedderson was being polite because of our personal relationship. As soon I was gone, a truckload of child actors would probably be arriving.

Whatever the case, the pressure was on. I had to "deliver the goods" with my reading. I tried to focus on my audition scene, reading it over with my dad who was with me. At last, the oak wooden door to the boss's inner office opened, and the casting director ushered me in.

Fedderson sat behind a huge desk, glowering like a Supreme Court justice. He was a hulking man whose perpetually tanned faced and steel-framed glasses exuded money and power.

George Tibbles, the show's head writer, and Gene Reynolds, the director, were also present. I decided to focus my attention on Reynolds, mainly because he was the only one who seemed friendly. He was a former child actor himself, and I'm sure he knew what it was like to stand in my shoes.

After a bit of genial chitchat, I read with the casting director. When I finished, I glanced around the room, and everyone was grinning. That was a good sign. Still, Fedderson didn't leap up to shake my hand and tell me I've got the job. He sat on his throne, coyly silent. Reynolds thanked me for coming in, and it was time to leave the room.

As I was heading for the door, I mentioned that my family was leaving for a vacation in Palm Springs. The big boss suddenly spoke up and ordered me to wait in the outer office. I groaned silently. As much as I wanted to hear I got the part, I was anxious to hit the road for a holiday.

I sat down next to my dad in the outer office. A long fifteen minutes ticked by, and not a word was uttered by anybody. What in hell was happening? There must be a heated debate going on behind the closed doors, some voting for me and some against. At last, Fedderson emerged from his office.

He said, "Sorry about the wait, buddy. I've got a vacation home in Palm Springs, and, well, I had to look everywhere for these." He held up a jangle of keys. "Since Barry's going to be joining our family, I thought you might like to stay at my place." That was one sweet way to start a holiday.

A defining new chapter of my life began. I became a full-fledged member of *My Three Sons*, put under contract to play Ernie Thompson, the friend next door, for a whopping salary of three hundred dollars per show. It was a pittance compared to salaries today, even after accounting for inflation. I couldn't have cared less about the money, though. Becoming part of *MTS* and spending more time with my older brother was good enough for me.

My parents, needless to say, were ecstatic. It wasn't just the extra money to them; it was added bragging rights. They now had two kids working on one of the most popular TV sitcoms ever. What were the odds?

My character was introduced on the series in an episode called *My Friend Ernie*. I was Chip's new buddy and hung out at the Douglas house, annoying the heck out of Bub (William Frawley). That became an ongoing gag.

Being a series regular now, I had to attend studio school full-time, putting in three hours of studying a day. When I wasn't working on the set, I'd get my time done in one uninterrupted run. That was great. On other busier days, it took all day to get in my three hours, usually done in ten-to twenty-minute chunks. That was hell. You'd have your nose in a math book, trying to fig-ure out a problem, and then get called to come work. After the scene was done, you'd return to the math problem, get in a few more minutes of study, only to be called away again in another ten minutes. That was the routine until you cobbled together three hours of schooling.

The ringmaster of my helter-skelter education was Sally Hickerson, a seventy-year-old studio teacher who claimed to have tutored Mickey Rooney and Judy Garland at MGM back in the day. She was way past her prime now and easily flustered, a fact that my brother and I exploited to the max.

One of our favorite stunts was to march into the schoolroom, click our heels, raise our right hands in a mock-Nazi salute, and yell, "Heil Hickerson!" Our cruel little stunt would send her into a tizzy, and she'd reprimand us in a warbling Julia Child falsetto. I knew that I was being a little monster, but the disgusted look on Miss Hickerson's face was worth every page that I had to transcribe from *Webster's Dictionary* as punishment.

Schooling at the studio had another drawback: a shoddy, one-room classroom. Ever the penny pinchers, the produc-tion company built an unventilated cubicle for us on our sound-stage, right under Don Grady's dressing room. Grady was an accomplished musician and could play every instrument imaginable . . . all day long. I'd be trying to memorize the Constitution downstairs while Don would be stomping his foot upstairs, keeping time to a song. His floor, *our* ceiling. Eventually, Stan or I would grab a flagpole with Old Glory on it and ram it into our ceiling to quiet the thumping. That was another sin in our teacher's patriotic eyes, a real desecration of the American flag. We'd be copying Mr. Webster's book for hours after that. To this day, thanks to Don Grady's constant toe tapping, I can only decipher algebra in a 4/4 musical time.

CHAPTER 12

Ernie Becomes Famous

The basic template for every *MTS* episode started with a son having a problem (a girl, a job, a car, etc.). Over the course of the story, Dad's invisible guiding hand would lead his troubled boy to a solution, and the son would think he'd figured out things on his own. Since I was the "new kid next door," my character was used mainly as a supporting player in everyone else's story.

Eventually, an episode was written that focused on Ernie. Ironically, Tim Considine, the original oldest son who played Mike, wrote it. I replaced him a year later when he left the show. (More on that later.) The storyline had me spying on Mike and an old flame. Since James Bond films were becoming hugely popular, I donned a trench coat, popped out of trash cans, and skulked down alleys in my pursuit.

After that episode aired, my fan mail shot up. It was nice that the fans of the show seemed to notice and like me. The letters were a real ego boost. Occasionally, though, they were a bit disturbing, particularly if the letter contained a picture of a fan that purportedly was Ernie's "twin." It was usually a photo of some scrawny, genetically challenged kid who wore ugly oversized glasses and had gnarled buckteeth. I knew I wasn't in Cary Grant's league, but I just didn't see myself in these guys, either. It seemed like there was a nation of nerds breeding out in the heartland, and I had somehow become their leader.

I discovered another odd phenomenon about big-time TV fame: people confused the scripted character of Ernie with the real me. That can cause a lot of identity issues for any actor, no matter what age. I'm sure I embodied some of Ernie's personality. I was bright, articulate, and, in some situations, cocky like my TV alter ego. In real life, though, I was a pretty shy kid who had learned to "turn on" my personality in professional situations. As Barry, I had to work to overcome my reticence and be comfortable with new people. Suddenly, way more people knew me as Ernie, not Barry. It's like they recognized something about me that I didn't know. I found that schism unnerving. I'm not a psychologist, but that discord was most likely the root cause for some of the troubles I had later in my life.

Things got even more confusing back at public school, which I attended during hiatus between shooting seasons. Kids were either overtly nice, trying to court a celebrity, or downright hostile if Ernie didn't act the way they expected. Grade school is a jungle, and I suddenly felt naked among the ruthless natives.

Public school was good survival training, though. I learned to joke my way out of confrontations with bullies and to laugh off the mockeries. Humming the *My Three Sons* theme song while tapping their feet (re: the show's animated introduction) was a frequent taunt. Once a hallway clogged with kids parted for me like Moses at the Red Sea. As I walked forward, the students on either side of the hall tapped their toes and hummed my "favorite tune." I laughed it off on the outside, but inside I was crying.

Naturally, I complained to my parents about my newfound notoriety, but they insisted that I stay in public school. They felt that it was good for me to be with my peers. Easy for them to say; they weren't getting tapioca tossed at them in the cafeteria. In retrospect, my parents made exactly the right decision and that probably accounts for whatever sanity I've maintained. I certainly grew a thicker skin.

Now that Stan and I were working on the same hit TV show, the family coffer was filling up nicely, so we moved to the upper-middle-class enclave of Studio City in the San Fernando Valley. My parents bought a ranch-style house with four bedrooms, three baths, and a huge swimming pool. They liked the idea that it was located next to the Studio City Park, a place they hoped I could make a few new pals. I was finding that increasingly hard.

On the days when I wasn't working, I'd venture over to the playground on my bike, make a quick sweep through the park, watch the kids playing ball, and then ride back home without uttering a word to anybody. The more famous I got, the more tentative I was about walking up to strange kids.

I realized that making new friends would require a little creativity on my part. The Beatles had just exploded in America, so I joined the fan club and sent away for a Fab Four Fan Kit that included photos, buttons, and a long black Beatle-style wig. I thought that if I went to the park wearing my new Beatle wig and Beatle boots, it would be a cool look, something far different from Ernie. I'd be the envy of every kid on the playground.

Moments later, I was pedaling across the park on my lime-green Schwinn, the one with a long banana-shaped seat and high-backed sissy bar. My shiny black Beatle wig, held in place by an elastic band under the chin, crowned my head, and I was certain that I was a dead ringer for John or Paul, or at least Ringo. (Who was pretty nerdy after all.)

I skidded to a stop next to the basketball court, threw down the kickstand, and waited for heads to turn. They did. Within seconds, a bunch of jocks sporting crew cuts gathered around me and started laughing their asses off. One of the bigger kids lifted my wig off the top of my head, elevating it as high as the rubber strap under my chin would allow. That got a laugh from the kids. When he let go of the wig, the hairy mop snapped back down on my noggin, landing askew. The elastic band worked flawlessly, and that elicited howls. Mortified, I pedaled away from the jeers and catcalls. I rarely went back to the park after that.

My true childhood playground was the Desilu Studios where *MTS* was filmed. There was always something amazing to discover. One of the coolest places was a storage area where they kept old movie props, some of them dating back thirty years or more to when RKO owned the lot.

Amid the piles of forgotten treasures, I found the model buildings that simulated New York City in the classic film, *King Kong*. It was all there collecting dust: the Chrysler Building, the Broadway theaters, even the Empire State Building that Kong had climbed. When we weren't working on the set, my brother and I played our version of *Kong*, running amuck amid the miniature buildings and feeling as powerful as the great ape himself. One Monday morning we arrived at the studio, and the model buildings had vanished. We were told that the old props were thrown away to make room for newer ones. Holy crap, we were pissed. Those models were so cool. If I'd only had the foresight, I would have asked for all of New York City. They'd be worth a small fortune today on the movie memorabilia circuit. Steven Spielberg paid $60,500 in 1982 for the "Rosebud" sled from *Citizen Kane*. Can you imagine the dollar value of the Empire State Building from the original *King Kong*?

Another fun stop on the Desilu playground was an underground garage where they stored the 1920s gangster cars used in the TV series *The Untouchables*. Stan and I had a ball climbing in and out of these classic autos with their running boards, pretending to battle it out as Eliot Ness and Al Capone.

Another great pleasure was sneaking onto the Paramount Studios lot that was right next door to Desilu, literally. I already knew the layout of the studio, having worked there earlier and taken a tour of the place with Elvis in his limo. A rickety wooden fence was all that separated the two studio empires. Stan and I found a break in the barrier, which gave our unauthorized visits an added air of danger. Trespassing was well worth the risk, though, since Paramount had a huge Western town where *Bonanza* and many other cowboy sagas were filmed. The authentic frontier buildings, dirt streets, horse troughs, and wooden walkways sparked our imaginations. Imaginary gunfights were mandatory with every visit. Paramount also had an enormous water tank (and still does) that could float an entire pirate ship when it was filled. That was a sight to behold.

Lunch at either studio commissary was always a mind-bending spectacle. It was a freak show of costumed actors working on *Star Trek*, *Hogan's Heroes*, *My Favorite Martian*, *Mission Impossible*, and *Lassie*. You'd see purple aliens dining with Navajos or country spinsters breaking bread with baldheaded KGB agents.

After living in our new home for about six months, I finally made friends with a neighbor boy, Jack McCalla. Whenever I wasn't working, we played "army" for hours, digging trenches and building forts. Once we dug a pit so deep, we buried a huge wooden crate in the hole, and it became our subterranean head-quarters. We stocked it with rations, installed a toy periscope to spy on the enemy soldiers above ground, and slept there on many summer nights, sweating it out like real "dogs of war" in our unventilated fort. We abandoned the bunker after winter rains flooded the place . . . and a few rats moved in to salvage our soggy rations.

There was another force in the world that was reshaping my views and my tastes: the English rock-and-roll invasion. Person-ally, I identified with the blossoming youth rebellion. Publicly, my wholesome alter ego, Ernie Douglas, was depicting me as a very different person. A new identity schism was brewing.

The kids at school and on the playground saw me as an agent of the "old guard." I was ostracized because my TV twin was more pervasive than the real me. As Ken Kesey said, "You were either on the bus or off the bus." Barry wanted to be "on the bus" but I kept getting recognized as Ernie and thrown off. As far as I could see it was a case of mistaken identity.

Trying to keep with the changing times, I begged my mom to get me a guitar like my new rock-and-roll heroes. She did, mainly because music lessons fit in with her cherished vision of me as a *well-rounded performer.*

My first and only guitar teacher was a sixteen-year-old prodigy, Gil Reigers, who later became Johnny Mathis's guitarist and arranger. Gil taught me to play the current hits like "I Want to Hold Your Hand" and "Blowing in the Wind" as well as classical Flamenco guitar, and I got pretty good.

I was even asked to perform on *Art Linkletter's House Party,* a very popular live daytime show. This was my first guitar performance, on live network TV no less, and my jitters made my fingers freeze up. Luckily, Linkletter blabbed on about my lengthy acting credits while I was playing "Malaguena," and the audience couldn't tell how badly I mangled it . . . I hope.

Like many other teens in the 1960s, rock-and-roll music fueled my fantasies of rebellion against authority. I even started to bristle against my mom's notion that I become the new Danny Kaye, that good old-fashioned song and dance man. I told my mom that I never saw Mick Jagger do a "shuffle-off-to-Buffalo" tap dance step.

Of course, my protests fell on deaf ears and I was soon enrolled in a new local performing arts school, the Eddie Gay Dance Academy. It was tough enough to study jazz and ballet, but telling kids that I was a member of the Eddie Gay Dance Academy really sucked, no offense to any homosexual fans. I went along with my mom's program, but in my head I knew that my dancing days were numbered.

CHAPTER 13

My Pal, Lucille Ball

 Back at work on *MTS* at Desilu, I started to become pals with the studio's owner, Lucille Ball. Lucy had divorced Desi Arnaz and had taken over the daily grind of running the place. That was in addition to producing and acting in *The Lucy Show*. She was a force of nature and seemed to be at the studio night and day.

After I'd finished school, I'd take a ride on my Schwinn, and my path frequently crossed with Lucy's, who was speeding around the lot in her golf cart. Since she wasn't in front of a camera, Lucy wore little or no makeup and would have her bright red hair tucked under a bandanna. A cigarette was also perpetually glued to her lower lip.

I couldn't believe my ears the first time she waved to me in passing, yelling out, "Hi there, Barry!" I practically fell off my bike. It was one thing when your average fan greets you and quite another when a world-famous celebrity and comedic legend knows your name. My afternoon encounters with Lucy continued on a daily basis, nothing more than passing smiles and waves. One day, though, it got more up close and personal.

One of my current passions was baseball, and I would spend hours bouncing a tennis ball off the wall of our soundstage, playing catch with myself. I didn't realized that my ball was also leaving little round smudge marks on the stage every time it hit it, which was hundreds of times. Lucy's new husband and business partner, Gary Morton, caught me in the act and went ballistic.

Morton screamed, "Kid, what the hell are you doing? Look at all those marks! It's gonna cost me a lot of money to repaint the side of that stage!"

Lucy pulled up next to us in her golf cart as Morton continued to rant and rave. "Gary, calm down for Chrissake. He's just a kid!" Lucy yelled.

Morton replied, "Somebody's gonna pay for this damage!"

"We'll pay for it!" Lucy growled in her gravelly voice. "Now shut up and get in the goddamn cart, Gary. We're late for a meeting!"

Morton did as ordered and climbed aboard, silently fuming.

Lucy turned to me and said, "Keep playing ball, honey, one day you'll be on the Dodgers." She stepped on the cart's accelerator pedal and sped away.

Even though Lucy generously gave me permission to play ball against her stage wall, I decided to get a "pitch-back" net to play catch with rather than tick off Lucy's surly partner. Not long after this incident, though, I ran afoul of Morton again.

Stan and I were racing our bikes down one of the studio avenues. We made a high-speed turn at an intersection, and I collided head-on with one of the scrawny feral cats that roamed the lot. Releasing the hungry felines was Morton's bright idea to control the rat population. I had accidentally run over one of his prized tomcats, snapping its neck and killing it instantly. Stan and I panicked and decided to hide the evidence. We tossed the dead cat under our soundstage and fled from the scene of the crime, thinking we'd dodged a bullet.

All was fine in the "case of the dead tomcat" until about a week later. A horde of flies invaded our set. You'd be filming a scene, having a heart-to-heart moment with MacMurray, when a big horsefly would orbit your head and land on your nose, ruining the take.

For the next week, scene after scene was ruined by the flying intruders, costing the company thousands in wasted film. Eventually, some poor soul was sent under the stage and found the decomposing cat. Stan and I maintained our silence and never confessed to our crime. Gary Morton, probably suspecting I was involved in the mystery, continued to give me the "stink eye" at every opportunity.

I wasn't so sure of my relationship with Lucy now that her husband seemed to hate me. My fears were soon put to rest when my agent called to say that Mrs. Ball had personally requested me for an episode of *The Lucy Show*. I was certainly available.

The episode was called "Lucy Gets Locked in a Vault," and I was to play Arnold Mooney, son of the bank president, Theodore Mooney, who was Lucy's boss. The story had Lucy demonstrating her frugal ways by giving me a homemade haircut, which accidentally comes out like a Mohawk.

When they filmed the scene, I sported a tall, bushy wig. Lucy and Vivian Vance, her longtime acting partner, stood in front of me blocking the live audience's view while I was being sheared. When they stepped aside and the Mohawk was revealed, the audience went wild. Lucy knew comedy.

A while later, Lucy requested me for another episode, "Lucy and the Scout Trip," and I returned to play Arnold Mooney again. I definitely landed on her "hire" list because a few more requests for my services popped up over the next few years. Unfortunately, I couldn't oblige because I was working on *MTS* full-time.

CHAPTER 14

Bub and Uncle Charley

 As sweet as Lucy was, Vivian Vance seemed like a grouch to work with. Maybe I caught her at a bad time. William Frawley (Bub on *MTS*) had nothing good to say about her, though. He played Vance's husband, Fred Mertz, on *I Love Lucy* for six seasons. Whenever her name came up, Frawley would blurt out his favorite description: "she's a double-barreled asshole."

I was told that Frawley and Vance got off on the wrong foot right at the beginning of their relationship. During an early casting session of *I Love Lucy*, Vance had a meeting with Lucy and Desi. When they informed her that they had hired William Frawley to play her husband, she blurted, "Oh, c'mon! Nobody would believe I'd be married to that old fart!" She didn't realize that Frawley was in a nearby room and overheard her comment.

He obviously never forgave her and transferred that real-life bitterness into their TV marriage. It was funny as hell on screen because the feelings were real.

Even though Frawley hadn't worked with Vance on *Lucy* for years, he held a grudge like an elephant. Occasionally, he would recruit Stan and me to help him harass Vance while she was working on the soundstage next to ours. When Frawley was in the mood for a sneak attack, usually after a few shots of Cutty Sark whiskey at lunch, we'd gather our ammunition: large circu-

lar film cans. Frawley would hold open *The Lucy Show* stage
door and cock his ear, listening to a scene being rehearsed inside. The second he heard Vivian's shrill voice he'd give us the
signal to fling the metal cans through the open door. They would
land with a loud metallic bang, and Frawley would yell, "Let's
get the hell out of here!" We'd flee like three juvenile delin-
quents, Frawley leading the way.

If Frawley liked you, though, he could be surprisingly thought-
ful. Example: when the surfing craze took off in the early sixties,
the old guy heard that Stan was excited about the new fad. Soon
after, a beautiful, expensive long board arrived as a present to
my brother. Pretty sweet.

As most fans of *MTS* know, Frawley's character, Bub, was the
family housekeeper and cook. If you look closely, though, you'll
notice that the old guy was totally inept in his duties. He was a
lifelong bachelor and probably couldn't bake a casserole to save
his life. Frawley would bark out his lines in a kitchen scene, all
the while knifing a loaf of bread like Jack the Ripper; the crust
would fly in every direction. When it came to folding laundry,
he'd crumple shirts in a loose wad and toss them aside in a
heap. I think people overlooked a lot of Frawley's gaffes because
they knew he was just being himself.

Frawley was Frawley on the set and off, speaking his mind
when others would just keep quiet. A perfect example was when
the show *This Is Your Life* devoted an episode to Frawley. The
program was shot live, and the idea was to ambush an unsuspecting celebrity, usually at a restaurant or a nightclub, and
then haul the honoree over to a studio where key people from
the celebrity's past would be trotted out for a reunion. In Frawley's show, camera crews and the show's host, Ralph Edwards,
surprised him at one of his favorite watering holes, The Brown
Derby, after he'd already guzzled three or four stiff drinks.
According to John Stephens, who was with him and in on the
ruse, Frawley's reaction was loud and blunt: "What the hell is
going on?!"

Things went downhill from there. Frawley was dragged bitching and moaning from his cozy booth at the restaurant to a
nearby studio filled with an audience to greet old friends and
acquaintances. Virtually every person that emerged from behind a curtain—grade school pals, old vaudevillians, former
girlfriends—Frawley didn't recognize. They'd sit next to the
guest of honor, recount their beloved memory of him, and
Frawley would reply, "I don't remember that, I don't remember
you at all!" The show's final, surprise guest was none other than
Frawley's ex-wife, the only person he did remember, because he
hated her! When the lady wrapped him in a fond embrace,
Frawley's puffy face turned reddish purple and he nearly passed
out from anger. Needless to say, the show required massive edit-
ing to weed out his muttered obscenities. What a hilarious
disaster.

Frawley was one tough guy, but old age and alcohol abuse
finally wore him down. It was painful to see him forget his lines.
One muffed take would follow another, and he'd try to cover his
embarrassment by bellowing, "Who writes this crap, anyway?"

Other problems started cropping up, too. If the company
didn't get Frawley's work filmed in the mornings, he might nod
off right in the middle of a scene by the afternoon. Eventually, a
prop man had to lie on the floor, out of the camera's view, and
tap on Frawley's shoe to keep him from dozing off during his
close-ups.

As season number five on *MTS* was about to commence,
Frawley was so frail he couldn't pass his health insurance exam.
All TV series regulars, no matter what age, must pass an insurance physical before every shooting season to verify they are in
good health and won't cause a costly shutdown of production if
they get sick. Apparently, Frawley's doctor couldn't even detect
his heart pulse.

The producers made the painful decision that it was too risky
for him to come back to work. Bub would have to be written out
of the series. Frawley was deeply hurt when he learned he had

to be let go. Despite the bad news, Frawley graciously returned to do a number of episodes that would explain his leaving the show; Bub was going to return to his native Ireland.

Frawley's departure poised a real risk to *MTS*. Anytime a popular character leaves a show, the ever-elusive chemistry that makes a series work is jeopardized. Initially, veteran actor James Gregory (later the chief of police in *Barney Miller*) came on to the show as Bub's brother. His deal called for him to do a number of episodes as a trial run. Turned out that Gregory hated the job of being the nanny and was soon gone. Next to be tested was William Demarest, a well-respected character actor, who would play Uncle Charley. Demarest was also MacMurray's personal friend. That bode well for his chances of staying, assuming he wanted to.

When Demarest arrived for work, Frawley was just finishing his final show. There was obvious tension between the "new boy" coming on board and the "old guy" leaving. Frawley and Demarest had been lifelong rivals, vying for the same roles in films over the years. Both men excelled at playing comic tough guys because that's what they were. Below their hard surface, though, they were very different people. Frawley was a lifelong bachelor, a heavy drinker, and profane as hell. Demarest was a devoted husband, sober as a preacher, and rarely swore. Despite their hard feelings, both men were stone-cold pros and got on with their jobs.

When Frawley's last day on the set arrived, it was tough to watch. Bub was saying good-bye to his TV family as much as to the actors who were his friends in real life. He passed away a few months after he left the show. Old age, hard living, and a broken heart took its toll.

Work proceeded on *MTS* with the new nanny, Uncle Charley. It was an edgy transition for the younger members of the cast, going from one crusty veteran housekeeper to the next. Despite his cantankerous nature, Frawley knew how to develop a rapport with kids and charm them. Demarest was more reserved and uneasy. Granted, he was coming into a difficult situation, being the "new kid on the block." Over time, though, we grew to accept him for who he was, a crusty old vaudevillian with endless stories about his "early days" in show business, playing cello, singing and dancing onstage in the boondocks. He also loved to talk about his relationship with Preston Sturges, one of Hollywood's first great auteurs, and how he got cast in the film *The Great McGinty.* According to Demarest, Sturges was at lunch one day with a friend, bemoaning the fact that he hadn't found the right actor for the key role of Skeeters, a hard-boiled campaign chief, and the film was about to start shooting. Further into their meal, the friend told Sturges a very, very dirty joke. When the director asked who told him such a foul knee-slapper, the man replied: William Demarest. Sturges immediately blurted out, "He's my Skeeter!" Demarest was immediately hired and went on to work with the great director in many of his other classics such as *The Lady Eve, The Miracle of Morgan's Creek, Sullivan's Travels,* and *The Palm Beach Story.*

I tried for many years to get Demarest to repeat the infamous nasty joke that endeared him to Sturges. He never would tell it to me, though, saying it was too "blue" for my young ears. That was the kind of man he was, a tough guy but with a strict moral compass around us youngsters. Frawley, uncensored and full of bluster, was much more fun.

I finally began to bond with Demarest when we filmed the cake-fight episode, one of my favorites. The story centered on a bakery business that Robbie was running out of the Douglas family home. Things get out of hand when his employees, the Douglas family and the neighborhood kids, have an enormous cake fight that destroys the business. Demarest, an old pro from vaudeville, really knew how to "take a pie in the face," a fact that impressed me greatly. He was pushing seventy and seemed to enjoy the messy chaos as much as I did.

Movie pie fights are choreographed ballets, designed to start slow and then build into a frenzied free-for-all. Here is the way we did it: The pie fight started when a neighbor kid shoved me and my arm landed in a freshly baked pie. In retaliation, I grabbed a cupcake and tossed it at the neighbor kid, but accidentally hit Chip instead. From that point on, the pattern is repeated: someone is provoked, they retaliate and accidentally hit an innocent bystander who gets sucked into the fray. The fight expands exponentially until chaos reigns.

One fact about pie fights: it's much more fun throwing the pies than it is getting hit. It's not the fruity goop that's the problem; it's the hard crust that hits your face like the slap of an open palm. The first time you're slammed, you are stunned and dazed. When the director asks for another take, then another, it's hard not to anticipate the pain of the exploding crust, particularly when a smirking prop man, enjoying his job a little too much, is launching it from off screen.

By the end of the day, we had filmed all the little moments leading up to the grand finale: a pie fight free-for-all. Now we were ready for one last take, and all hell was going to break loose. Three cameras were set up to capture the action. There would be no second takes, because we were going to throw everything but the furniture at each other. Cool.

The director yelled "action," and it was a cake-throwing shit-storm. The floor got so coated with goop that I slipped and fell. Demarest saw me sitting on my ass and took advantage, planting a huge metal bowl of icing over my head. I remember him laughing his ass off, having caught me with my guard down. What a joker. I practically choked to death on Betty Crocker's frosting mix. The pain was worth every second, though. What a crazy, wonderful way to make a living.

CHAPTER 15

Ernie to the Rescue

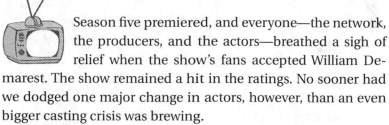 Season five premiered, and everyone—the network, the producers, and the actors—breathed a sigh of relief when the show's fans accepted William Demarest. The show remained a hit in the ratings. No sooner had we dodged one major change in actors, however, than an even bigger casting crisis was brewing.

Tim Considine, who played the oldest son Mike, wanted to direct more episodes of *MTS*. He had already done one and wanted additional assignments. Unfortunately, Considine's request to helm additional shows challenged the status quo: the MacMurray Method. That process required filming scenes from five to ten scripts a day, with one director to ensure continuity. Allowing other directors to helm an episode here and there would wreak havoc on the system. The only other option was to hire Considine as the full-time director to do every episode in a season. That wasn't likely, either. Fred was happy with the way things were.

With his contract expiring, Considine met with Don Fedderson and John Stephens, the show's producers, to make his position clear. He yearned for more challenges as an artist and told his employers that he was reluctant to renew his acting contract if his directing aspirations were not met. It was a gamble that Considine must have felt he could win. The show was called *My*

Three Sons after all. If he left, what were they going to do, re-name it *My* Two *Sons*?

Without tipping his hand, Fedderson told Considine that he'd have to think things over. The moment Considine was out the door, Fedderson turned to Stephens and said, "It looks like we'll have to write him out of the show." Case closed.

Apparently, there was another factor behind the quick cast-ing decision, and it involved MacMurray, the real power behind the throne. He was okay with giving Considine his one opportu-nity to helm an episode. The star was not comfortable with his "son" directing him in any future episodes, though. One shot was it, even though Considine had done a terrific job. The "oldest son" was welcome as an actor but not as one of the show's on-going directors. Call it ego or whatever. That's what MacMurray wanted, and that's the way it would be.

If losing a "son" wasn't a big enough problem, the producers were confronted with an even bigger bombshell. ABC, the net-work airing the series, decided to drop the show even though *MTS* was still drawing audiences of thirty million. The brains at ABC were betting that the show's future was limited, and a costly new deal with Mac-Fedd Productions (MacMurray/Fed-derson) was not worth the risk, especially if the show was losing a very popular player like Considine.

Don Fedderson had two other options to resell the show: NBC and CBS. The rounds were made, deals were tendered, and CBS rolled the dice and bought the series outright from Mac-Fedd Productions. MacMurray and Fedderson pocketed a princely five million dollars (approx. $50 million by today's standards) in the process. Switching networks rarely happens on TV. Nobody really likes "yesterday's papers." Nonetheless, CBS gave *MTS* a new home despite the fact that the show needed an-other major rewrite to introduce a new "son." Question was . . . where do you get a new "son"?

When the starting pitcher leaves in the middle of a baseball game, the manager looks to the bullpen. That's how my reputation in TV was built, like a relief pitcher. Ozzie Nelson tapped me to replace Stan when he left his show, and now the producers of *MTS* saw me on their roster of talent to take over Considine's starting position.

It was a stunning and delightful moment when the producers informed my family of their plans to make me a full-fledged "son." I personally hated to see Considine leave. He was a very cool guy, and I looked up to him for outspokenness and his irreverent sense of humor. He also shared with me his love of auto racing, not to mention his great seats at Dodger games. Nonetheless, he was leaving to pursue other endeavors, which left a giant hole in the lineup. (Tim would make movie history in a couple more years when he played the stressed-out soldier George C. Scott slaps silly in the 1970s *Patton.*)

I'd been on the show for about a year and a half as the friend next door. In all that time nobody told me that I was a foster child. That was the angle the producers were going to use to bring me into the show as a full-time member. I was available for adoption when my foster parents (again, people I had never seen in my previous years) were leaving the country and couldn't take me with them. Rather than let Ernie disappear into an orphanage, the Douglas family would take him in. Thus, the show's title, *My Three Sons*, would still be valid and the franchise preserved.

Ernie's adoption process occurred over a six-episode arc. If you were hiking in the jungle and missed seeing those shows, you wouldn't have a clue as to how I became a son, because my adoption was never mentioned again.

The tone of *MTS*, lighthearted and whimsical, took a turn toward the dramatic during my induction to the family. Some quasi-serious issues had to be addressed: Could cranky old Uncle Charley prove to the adoption board that he could be a nurturing surrogate mom? When could I start calling Steve Douglas "Dad"? What are we going to do with my dog, Wilson, since the family already had a hound named Tramp? Once all these transitional problems were addressed, life got back to normal on the show. My foster parents, and Considine's character, were gone forever. *MTS* was a sweet and wholesome world on screen; off screen it was all business.

The sixth season of *My Three Sons* premiered on CBS, and the show's ratings soared. Demarest and I had to fill the shoes of two popular original cast members, and, thankfully, the fans accepted us.

One of my favorite episodes was filmed after I became a "son," and it involved working with a lion. The story called for the beast to take refuge in the Douglas house after escaping from a circus that was visiting our midwestern town, Bryant Park. It was always funny to the *MTS* actors that our fictional little city had everything that a major metropolis would have: an international airport, a thriving Chinatown and a Little Italy, visiting movies stars, a major aeronautical industry (fyi: Steve Douglas was an aeronautical engineer). Nobody ever gave it a second thought.

In the lion episode, Ernie was the first person to spot the errant big cat lolling around in the backyard. When I tell "Dad" about the beast, he thinks I'm making things up to get attention since I was just adopted. Eventually, everybody has a run-in with the lion as it roams about the house. It was a pretty amusing show. The most memorable part about that episode was what happened off screen when the heavily sedated cat got loose from his cage.

Panic ensued when we learned that the lion was roaming free on our soundstage. The place was as big as a blimp hangar and had many dark areas for a predator to hide in. The crew huddled together in a brightly lit area of the stage, and Stan and I hid in our schoolroom while the trainer hunted for the big cat.

Meanwhile, Demarest arrived for work, unaware of the crisis, and entered the dimly lit stage. Once the old guy's eyes adjusted to the darkness, he took a few steps and then stopped; the lion stood in front of him, about ten feet away. He knew the animal was working that day, but he didn't expect to see him hanging out all by himself. Something was definitely wrong with that picture.

Demarest turned and ran like a teenager. The lion's predatory instincts kicked in, and he gave chase. Luckily, the actor's dressing room was close by. He outran the lion and dashed into his room, slamming the door in the big cat's face. Demarest got on the phone and called the authorities to tell them where they could find the missing cat: right outside his door. He wasn't a guy prone to cursing, but on this occasion, he cut loose with a vulgar volley that would have made William Frawley blush.

CHAPTER 16

The CBS Years and
Fred De Cordova

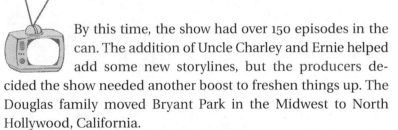 By this time, the show had over 150 episodes in the can. The addition of Uncle Charley and Ernie helped add some new storylines, but the producers decided the show needed another boost to freshen things up. The Douglas family moved Bryant Park in the Midwest to North Hollywood, California.

The shift in locale meant we would be filming at a new studio, the CBS production facilities in Studio City. It was a whole new playground to explore. There was the *Gilligan's Island* lagoon to check out. The new studio also had a sprawling Western town where *Wild, Wild West, Gunsmoke,* and *Big Valley* filmed. The move also brought a new and important person into my life: Fred De Cordova, our next director.

Frederick Timmins De Cordova was a legend in Hollywood, not so much for the B movies he directed like *Bedtime for Bonzo* or *Frankie and Johnny,* but for his razor-sharp wit, charisma, and close connections with people in the upper echelons of society. When he was a young man he attended Harvard and sharpened his verbal skills as a regular attendee at the infamous Algonquin Round Table in New York where the brilliant minds of the day, George S. Kaufman, Dorothy Parker, and Noel Coward, gathered to spar with their witticisms. Now in his mid-fifties, De Cordova's personal friends included Ronald Reagan,

James Mason, Walter Annenberg (founder of *TV Guide*), the Shuberts of Broadway, George Burns, and Bob Hope. His closest pal was Jack Benny, whose Emmy award–winning television show he produced and directed.

I had never seen or heard anybody like him. I immediately fell under his spell, enamored by his sophistication and charm. Woe to anybody, cast or crew, who messed up, for they became immediate fodder for a De Cordova put-down. Defending yourself was useless; his sharp tongue could cut a challenger's ego to pieces in seconds. Even MacMurray seemed intimidated and was not spared from his acerbic quips.

I'm not sure what De Cordova saw in me, but we bonded fast. Perhaps I was a surrogate son he never had. Whatever the case, De Cordova became my best new pal and role model.

The instant I finished my studio schooling for the day, I'd make a beeline to wherever he was. We'd talk about sports, movies, or headlines, and I'd try to make him laugh with my own sarcastic quips, imitating the master. After the day's work was done, we'd hop onto his flaming-red golf cart, dubbed Mr. D's Dragon, and race up to his office. He'd make himself a vodka martini, I'd grab a Coke, and we'd head for a screening room to view the dailies. Half the time we'd make jokes about the other actors, laughing at their quirks that were so naked and exposed in the rough uncut footage. After the dailies, he'd chauffeur me home in his Cadillac, the only brand he'd drive. Then he'd race away to spend the rest of the evening at some elegant soiree up where a Kennedy or a Rockefeller was being feted. It was just another average day in the life of Frederick Timmins De Cordova.

One day De Cordova invited me to go with him to a Dodgers game. Naturally, he knew the team's owner, Peter O'Malley, and had the best seats. Game day arrived, and I was hoping to leave early for the park to watch batting practice. Fred told me to relax, that we had to wait for a friend of his who would be going with us. The doorbell rang, and Fred ordered me to get it.

I did my best De Cordova imitation and huffed, "What do I look like, a servant?" The doorbell rang again, and Fred insisted that I open the door.

This time I obeyed. I opened the door, and Jack Benny was standing there. "Well, you're a bit young to be a butler, aren't you?" he said.

I shot back, "And you're a bit old to be selling Avon." Ba-da-boom! As I had hoped, both men laughed, especially De Cordova, and that was all that ever mattered.

Driving to the ballpark, I soaked in the conversation between these two funny men. One particularly funny moment came when Benny started to describe an encounter with the son of Vin Scully, the Dodgers announcer.

Benny said, "Fred, I can't tell you how much Vinnie's kid looks just like his old man. I swear, if I were lost in a snow storm in Alaska, and I came upon an igloo, and inside that igloo I saw a family of Eskimos sitting around a fire, eating whale blubber, and in their midst I saw this redheaded kid, I would say '*That's Vin Scully's son!*'" Benny's timing was impeccable.

Once we got to the exclusive Club Level of the stadium, De Cordova, Benny, and I were escorted to Peter O'Malley's private box. I was in Dodgers heaven, gorging on free Dodgers dogs, ice cream, Cokes, and hanging out with two of the funniest men on the planet while watching my favorite baseball team from the best seats in the house.

After the game, De Cordova drove the three of us in his Caddie to the eastern end of the Sunset Strip and the old Cock and Bull Restaurant. We finished the day with massive steak dinners and drinks, martinis for the men and a tall Roy Rogers for me. It was another typical day in the life of De Cordova, and a pretty amazing one for me.

A few feature films were coming on to the CBS studio lot to film and, naturally, De Cordova knew all the stars involved. We'd march onto any soundstage like De Cordova owned the place, disregarding the Closed Set sign on the door meant to keep out visitors. Jack Lemmon was shooting *The April Fools* and greeted us like family, whipping out pricey cigars. Lee Marvin, filming *Monte Walsh*, roared with glee at the sight of De Cordova, and we retired to the actor's dressing room for a quick cocktail. Even the young anti-establishment star Dustin Hoffman, who was working on *Little Big Man*, was savvy enough to leap up from his chair to honor the presence of *Mister* De Cordova.

The De Cordova era of *MTS* ushered in another big change in the show: women. The Douglas family had always been an all-male household, one of the more unique and charming aspects of the show. For a series to last as long as *MTS*, though, change was inevitable. It certainly made sense for the older sons to consider getting married. At least it put to rest some of the taunts at my public school that the Douglases were all "closet homos."

The first girl to be a series regular was Tina Cole, who played Katie, Robbie's wife. Since Robbie was still in college, the newlyweds lived at the Douglas family house. This opened up a whole new batch of storylines with a woman in the house. It also opened up some other questions about the honesty of the show, particularly about sex. In the real world, the contraceptive "pill" had altered society's views about fornication. It was now a recreational activity. The taboos related to religion and accidental pregnancies were fading away. Despite these changes, CBS insisted that Robbie and Katie's bedroom be furnished with twin beds. What young, healthy married couple in the mid-sixties slept in twin beds? Not many. The censors surmised that just the sight of a king-size bed inferred lusty comingling. That was unthinkable in their 1950s mind-set. The media cretins calling the shots also chose to ignore most other changes that were happening in America, too. The civil rights movement, the Vietnam War, and the nuclear arms race with the Russians were all happening in a land far, far away from the peaceful world of *My Three Sons*.

To Don Grady's (Robbie) credit, he did some research on the "twin bed" issue. He found out that *Bewitched,* another popular sitcom of that era, had broken the bedroom code. Darrin and Samantha, the married couple on that show, were recently allowed to have a king-size mattress in their bedroom. With that precedent achieved, the CBS censor caved . . . with one caveat: Robbie and Katie can never be seen under the covers at the same time, and if one of them was already under the blankets, the other had to be in full pajamas standing outside of the bed or sitting on it. Whew. The virgin minds of young Americans were spared another trauma by our clever and vigilant media watchdogs.

CHAPTER 17

Making a Best Friend, Losing a Best Friend

 When I returned to public school, the radical cultural changes (civil rights, Vietnam, hippies) unfolding in America were obvious. More than ever I felt like the poster boy for the dreaded "establishment." I went from being a regular celebrity to an *uncool* celebrity, like Richard Nixon or Lawrence Welk. Mockery was shifting to outright scorn. That really hurt. There was no bucking the power of TV to reinforce an image, be it true or false. I felt pretty isolated.

One of my problems making friends at school stemmed from the fact that I wasn't on campus long enough to connect with other kids. My work schedule kept me at the studio for a good part of the year.

I'd also become more comfortable hanging out with adults than my peer group. Kids could be unpredictable if not downright mean. That kind of social disconnect is pretty common among most child stars and, no doubt, accounts for some dysfunctional behavior as they reach adulthood. It's pretty clear to see that now, with the benefit of time and a lot of psychoanalysis. When I was a teenager, though, it felt like a whole lot of inexplicable, hostile rejection.

It was no surprise that my social life was pretty dull. I'd even outgrown my one good neighborhood pal and "army" buddy, Jack McCalla. War games weren't as fun now that gory images from the Vietnam War appeared on the TV news every night. Occasionally, I'd tag along with my brother Stan and his gang to cruise Sunset Strip for chicks. We'd usually wind up for breakfast at the International House of Pancakes at two in the morning alongside such burgeoning rock-and-rollers as Neil Young, Jim Morrison, and David Crosby having their after-the-gig meals. It was great hanging out with the older guys, but I always felt like I was a junior member of the pack and could be expelled at any moment.

I did have one great, reliable friend to keep me company when I was alone: the Los Angeles Dodgers. I'd lock myself in a bathroom at our house and listen to the games on my transistor radio. I was like Superman in his Fortress of Solitude, making notes on the players' stats, hanging on Vin Scully's words as he'd describe the play-by-play action. Dodger games were my holy hours. I was not to be disturbed, particularly if my hero, Sandy Koufax, was pitching the game. I was alone but never lonely when the game was on.

It wasn't until I graduated from Millikan Middle School and entered North Hollywood High that I connected with a few kindred spirits. The first great friend I made was Gene King. He was initially a buddy of my brother Stan, who met him while they were attending North Hollywood High.

Gene was a fifteen-year-old speed-talker, a raconteur and a dead ringer for Gene Clark, the lead singer of the Byrds. His parents were alcoholics and abusive, and he sought refuge at our house on the weekends. Very quickly, Gene and my mother bonded over pots of Yuban coffee and unfiltered Pall Mall cigarettes.

Over the summer of 1968, Gene went from a kid who occasionally slept over to a full-time member of our family. My parents had a rocky husband-wife relationship, but they were in total sync when it came to sheltering kids in need. They'd already adopted two children at birth, my brother Bill and my sister Michelle. Now Gene joined our brood. It was one big happy family on Milbank Street until Stan unleashed a bomb-shell: he was getting married and would be moving out of the house.

Stan was seventeen years old when he told my parents that he had met his future bride on a late-night outing at the Pan-cake House. Enter Sandy Goble. She was four years older than Stan and was working as a "cage dancer" at the Whiskey-a-Go-Go nightclub. Naturally, my flustered parents disapproved and counseled my love-struck brother to wait. They tried to point out the risks of getting married so young, particularly to an older woman who was a *go-go-dancer* at the Whiskey.

My parents' warning fell on skeptical ears, though. Stan re-minded my mom that she ran away from her home in Beaver Falls at sixteen and worked as a "fan dancer." That pretty much destroyed their arguments to dissuade my brother.

I wasn't keen about Stan's marriage, because it meant losing my brother and best friend. From the beginning, Stan's future bride tried to pry him away from his family. To her defense, Sandy was not exactly welcomed with open arms by my mom and dad. I resented her greatly, much like Paul McCartney must have felt about losing John Lennon to Yoko Ono.

My parents obviously had another concern about Stan's im-pending marriage: the impact it would have on his career. Wholesome teenage Chip Douglas marrying a go-go-dancer from the Whiskey? What would CBS think? What would the American public think? What would *Fred MacMurray* think?

The series had been on for eight years, and certainly by now our relationship with MacMurray was established: it was all business. *My Three Sons* was just a workplace for the star, and we were his junior colleagues. When it came to personal issues, he stiffened and steered clear . . . unless your issue impacted the show. I was damned curious about MacMurray's reaction to Chip's real-life bride.

Stan introduced Sandy to MacMurray at a publicity function, and she was sporting her go-go-dancer look: short miniskirt, boots, long black wig that buried her face in hair, and thick black eyelashes. I think she was shooting for Priscilla Presley but looked more like Morticia of the Addams Family. It was impossible to miss MacMurray's shock and disapproval. He was a very conservative man, easily rattled by anything that smacked of counterculture or weird. The awkward handshake that ensued looked about as heartfelt as a family patriarch welcoming Elvira, Mistress of the Dark, into the family.

Soon after that meeting, MacMurray broke from his rule of avoiding personal issues and took Stan aside to voice his concerns. Stan responded with the "true love" speech, and Mac-Murray quickly retreated, sensing that he'd crossed his own line of ethics with his "boys." MacMurray said nothing more about Sandy and accepted the inevitable, like we all did.

The wedding took place at the Little Brown Church in Studio City, a chapel famous for quickie unions. Of the show's cast, only the "sons" attended the ceremony. Fortunately, the tabloid press, which today loves to shred celebrities for their missteps, was still in its infancy. Stan's teen marriage was pretty much overlooked by the press.

Seven years after it began, the marriage ended. Their union did produce something wonderful, though: a daughter named Samantha Livingston. She has grown up to be a beautiful woman who loves her dad unconditionally.

Now that Stan was out of our Milbank house, Gene and I became best friends. Gene was three years older than me but only a grade ahead in school, which was North Hollywood High. It wasn't that he was dumb; he just enjoyed the social whirl on campus. We made quite a pair. I was very serious about getting good grades and never cut classes. Gene, on the other hand, was dubbed the "phantom of the hallways" by the school's vice principal for his truancy reputation.

In tenth grade, I worked in the attendance office, and my job was to deliver messages to students during classes. More often than not, while I was walking about the campus delivering a summons, I'd encounter Gene bursting out of a boy's bathroom followed by a cloud of cigarette smoke. The "phantom," on the run as usual, would accompany me on my errand and then vanish into the next available bathroom hideout.

North Hollywood High had the dubious distinction of being the only campus in Los Angeles that didn't enforce a dress code or make you cut your hair. The place became a magnet for every teenage rock-and-roller and hippie freak in Southern California.

I showed my allegiance to the brave new world by letting my hair grow really long and dressing like a hippie, complete with love beads and leather-fringed vest. After years of feeling like I was walking around at school with a big scarlet letter, "E" for Ernie, on my forehead, I finally felt like I was fitting in.

Maybe I was just maturing and wasn't as sensitive to being made fun of. Maybe my peers were growing up, too, and weren't as eager to rub my squeaky-clean TV image in my face. More likely, everybody was just too stoned to care anymore. This was the late 1960s, after all.

The Times They Are A-Changin'

Going back to work on *MTS* for its eleventh season was tough for a couple of reasons. First, I was actually enjoying public school, and second, Fred De Cordova announced that he was leaving at the end of the upcoming season. My good pal was asked by Johnny Carson to produce his late-night TV program, *The Tonight Show.* With his showbiz and society connections, De Cordova was the perfect choice. My loss was certainly Carson's gain.

Work plodded along under a cloud. De Cordova was on his way out, and the show's episodes felt more dated and out of sync with the times than ever before. The real world was in turmoil with wars, social upheavals, and political scandals, yet we were still locked into stories about Ernie's lost dog or Chip's big science project.

The performances by the actors, adults, and kids alike began to feel rote, too. Even the addition of new characters such as Robbie and Katie's triplets, Steve Douglas's new wife, Barbara, and her daughter, Dodie, didn't add enough spark. No offense to the fine actors (Beverly Garland, Ronnie Troup, and Dawn Lyn) who came onto the show. It's just that these injections of life felt like booster shots being given to a terminal patient. The unique concept of the show, a single parent raising three boys in an all-male household, was long gone.

As shooting continued that year, more problems began to surface. Don Grady announced that he wouldn't be returning next season, assuming we'd be renewed. Grady had worked on the show for more than a decade and was ready to pursue his musical ambitions full-time. The veracity of the show's title, *My Three Sons,* was up in the air again.

William Demarest, now pushing eighty years old, was in fairly good health but having memory problems, forcing the writers to limit his dialogue.

MacMurray, too, was in his mid-sixties and showing impatience with his new TV daughter, Dodie. Dawn Lynn, the feisty little actress who played Dodie, occasionally liked to reach out and pull on Fred's toupee. That was a big no-no.

As for my character, I was the only "son" left in the house. Chip married Polly (Ronnie Troup) and was gone. Robbie, Katie, and the triplets had their own place, and Mike, well, nobody knew what the hell happened to him. The lack of children at home really undermined one of the show's basic charms: Mac-Murray's relationship with his boys. Dad had all that folksy wisdom and nobody to counsel anymore. The empty nest only exacerbated the dearth of creative storylines.

Around this time, a new television program exploded into the public eye: *All in the Family.* That cutting-edge, incendiary show was a dagger into the heart of our benign sitcom reality. *All in the Family* tackled topical issues such as the Vietnam War, unwanted pregnancies, and racial bigotry in a way that was as honest as it was funny. The cultural revolution that was taking place out on the streets had finally reached TV entertainment. The CBS censors really had their hands full now.

Despite the game-changing success of *All in the Family,* MTS stuck to its wholesome, nonthreatening format. The younger actors on *MTS* lobbied hard for more challenging, topical episodes, but the producers held steadfast to the original tone of the show. In retrospect, this was a wise decision.

It would have been a disaster for *MTS* to mimic Norman

Lear's new shows with their controversial storylines. If we had done so, Steve Douglas might have recommended to Katie that she should get an abortion rather than have the triplets. Uncle Charley would have come "out of the closet" and revealed he was gay. Ernie, depressed over his lost dog, might have overdosed on Barbara's Valiums.

Drastic changes in the *MTS* format wouldn't have worked in a million years. You can put ballet shoes on an elephant and call it a dancer, but it's still a plodding pachyderm any way you look at it. It was best to be true to what we were: sitcom dinosaurs from another era. Our fate was to keep on marching until we keeled over, extinct from exhaustion.

Fred De Cordova's last day of shooting arrived, and it was time to say good-bye. Everyone in the cast liked him, or at least respected him, but I loved him. I watched him speed away in his red golf cart, Mr. D's Dragon, and actually cried. I had the urge to give him one last farewell hug, and I ran after him, sobbing the whole way. I arrived at his office, but he wasn't there. In fact, the place was already empty. I couldn't believe how fast his private suite was cleared out. Then it really sunk in: my great friend, a guy I adored and emulated to a fault, was gone. He was off to New York and most likely never to be heard from again. That's showbiz.

I felt terrible and very lonely as I headed back to North Hollywood High for another semester. The future seemed so bleak. Then, things unexpectedly took a turn for the better. I met a girl.

CHAPTER 19

My First Girlfriend

Tina Harris. What a wildcat. I was totally unprepared for our emotional roller-coaster relationship.

Tina was my age, sixteen, and going on thirty-nine. She was a natural-blond Swede and built like one of Hugh Hefner's curvaceous wives. In contrast to her physical beauty, she was a wiseacre with a salty vocabulary delivered out of the side of her mouth. If we'd met in the 1940s, I would have called her a "broad" or "one swell dame." Her stunning looks and bawdy language always drew stares, especially from her horny teenage admirers. I was right there at the front of the pack, gawking and drooling.

I was no Brad Pitt, and I knew my chances of wowing her with my nerdy looks were pretty slim. It occurred to me that I did have one advantage over my competitors: fame. For the first time I was not shy about playing the celebrity card. Raging hormones were driving me to pull out all the stops. Just for the record, I was still a virgin and getting laid was a high priority. I'd had a few dates but had never ventured beyond kissing and some clumsy breast squeezing. I had to talk to this blond teen goddess.

My plan was to stand behind Tina in the lunch line, act all nonchalant, and hope to start a conversation. On my first attempt, the ploy worked. She glanced back at me, and I croaked "hello." To my surprise, she said *hiya!* and maintained her eye contact, waiting for me to say something else. Holy crap, I had done it; I achieved the unimaginable, I got her attention. Unfortunately, my tongue seized up. I searched for a few words, any kind of utterance at all that would end my brain freeze. None came.

Suddenly, Tina was tackled from behind by her screaming, giggling best friend, Helen. In a flash, she dragged Tina away, destroying our beautiful, albeit silent, moment. I'd have to switch to Plan B.

Gene knew the location of Tina's locker, so I thought I might be able to catch her there, give her a friendly wave, and hope for the best. I staked out the locker for days, but Tina was never there. I learned that pretty girls rarely need books to get through school, or life for that matter. I'd have to come up with another plan.

I recently got my driver's license, so I figured I'd borrow my mom's silver Lincoln Continental and park it in front of school. Cool rides are always chick magnets, and I hoped that the car's sexiness might rub off on me. It was nerd desperation at its lowest.

To make the plan work, I parked in front of school two hours before the morning bell so I could snag a prime, highly visible spot. This had to be true love; nothing else would have gotten me to school *that* early.

I waited and watched students arrive, but Tina didn't show. Damnit! That was two hours better off spent in bed. I figured I had another shot at letting her see me behind the wheel of the big Lincoln that afternoon, after school let out.

The final bell rang, and I made a dash to my silver chariot parked out in front of school and waited for Tina to appear.

Just like in a movie, she bounded down the steps of Kennedy Hall, and our eyes met. A faint smile played on her lips as she saw me sitting behind the wheel of that shiny, sexy vehicle. I felt like Mr. Cool as I waved for her to come over, offering her a ride. My heart raced as she started walking toward me.

Just as she neared my car, Helen blasted out of nowhere, bellowing like a moose in heat. Tina looked over at her pal, and the spell I was weaving was broken. Helen leaped on Tina like a giant octopus, wrapping her arms around her, and hauled her away, again. Like many teenage girlfriends, they were attached at the hip. I wondered where I could get a "hit man" to rub Helen out.

As luck would have it, my first moment alone with Tina happened by accident, while I was driving my dad's shit-brown, banged-up Chevy Caprice.

I came to a stop at a red light and saw Tina standing on the corner, waiting to cross the street. My head throbbed with an instant adrenaline rush. I beeped and offered her a ride.

She hesitated, thinking it over. As I waited for her decision, I half expected Helen's screaming head to pop out of a street manhole and spoil our chance meeting, once again. That thought may have crossed Tina's mind, too, because she darted for my car and hopped in.

Once we were able to have ten seconds alone with each other, we clicked immediately. I wound up driving Tina to her home, a triplex bungalow in a seedy section of North Hollywood. Her parents were divorced, and she lived with her seventy-year-old dad, a house painter by day and heavy drinker by night. That explained the contradiction between her world-class beauty and blue-collar personality.

We went from our first meeting to our first kiss quickly. I could tell she had a lot more practice at this than I did. No big surprise there, me being a virgin. We'd hang out at my house or drive to Leo Carrillo beach and smooch like mad, fueled by bottles of cheap red wine. I was eager to graduate from just petting to real sex. Tina, though, always pulled back when my pawing and clawing got a little too hot. That left me frustrated as hell, but I didn't push things. I was in love and trying to go with the flow, although the "flow" on my part was getting pretty stopped up.

After a few months of dating, another problem developed. Tina didn't have a driver's license, so I became her chauffeur-on-call whenever she needed a ride. I happily obliged because it was another opportunity to be with her. The fun started to wane when Tina began asking for rides to Gazzarri's Nightclub on the Sunset Strip . . . without inviting me to join her.

At first, it was no big deal for me to drive her to a nightclub every so often and not be asked to join her. Dancing wasn't my thing, so I was kind of relieved. Nonetheless, a token invitation would have been nice since we were going steady. Soon the occasional night out became an every weekend event; that's when I became worried and voiced my concerns. Tina laughed off my questions and described her evenings as a "girl's night out" with Helen. She told me I was just being paranoid. Absolutely. My fear was confirmed when I accidentally discovered her secret life in Hollywood.

After dropping Tina off at Gazzarri's one night, I went to visit with a photographer friend of mine. He lived right around the corner from the nightclub and shot pictures of famous rock-and-roll bands like the Doors, Steely Dan, and Van Halen. Looking through some of his picture albums, one photo jumped out: Tina, in the arms of a very popular rock star. She was sitting on the rock star's lap with her blouse wide open, breasts hanging out, and guzzling a beer. My photographer buddy didn't know that Tina and I were friends, and I certainly didn't know that she was one of the boldest, most successful groupies on the Sunset Strip . . . until my buddy told me.

Apparently, Tina would sleep with just about anybody with a shag haircut, leather pants, and an English accent. What a kick to the gut. Not only had I been lied to, Tina was having sex with everybody in town but me!

I exploded the next time I saw her, and Tina confessed to her secret life. She tried to calm my hurt feelings by claiming that sex with rock stars was meaningless. It was nothing more than "bragging rights" with her friends. Our love, on the other hand, was something special. She hoped that it would remain pure and last forever. This, obviously, is where we differed. I didn't want some kind of holier-than-thou relationship. I was hoping that things might get completely vile and nasty. *Something pure and special, my ass.* I wasn't Jesus, and she certainly wasn't the Virgin Mary.

After the dust settled, I forgave her. That's how horny and desperate I was at sixteen. Hope, and *boners,* spring eternal.

I continued driving her to the clubs on Sunset Strip. After I dropped her off, I'd kick myself all the way home for being such a hopeless wimp. I was just too young to face the facts: it's better to be single and all alone than to be in a relationship where you are treated like a chump.

Eventually, Tina saw that her "chauffeur" was disgruntled and about to quit. In a last-ditch effort to salvage things, she decided we should make love and take our "pure" relationship to a new level. What a disaster that was.

Our sex was without feeling and over in about twenty seconds. The "new level" that she spoke of was a trip to the basement for my male ego, which took years to recover. Like I said before, Tina liked to laugh, and I was her willing clown. You gotta start somewhere, I guess.

CHAPTER 20

A Kindred Spirit and Partner in Crime

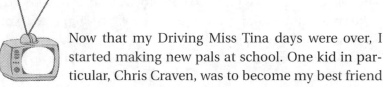

Now that my Driving Miss Tina days were over, I started making new pals at school. One kid in particular, Chris Craven, was to become my best friend and a huge influence on my life. Unlike most high school kids, Chris seemed worldlier and savvy. He turned me onto Jack Kerouac's books and knew about people like Ken Kesey and the Merry Pranksters up in San Francisco. Surprisingly few teens were aware of their influence on our changing world.

Chris and I also shared a love of old movies and theater. His dad, Eddie Craven, was a character actor under contract to Paramount Studios, and his uncles Frank and John were both Broadway stars, appearing in the original production of Thornton Wilder's classic play, *Our Town*.

I first noticed Chris when he was performing in a play at a school assembly. His performance really stood out, particularly an improvised moment at the end of the show that brought the teenage audience to its feet.

The play, a Japanese melodrama called *The Lost Princess*, starring my friend Gene and was performed in sign language in the Kabuki tradition. It was a nice idea to present something different, but the drama teacher badly overestimated the patience of her audience. Everybody was bored to tears by the show. Most of the kids at North Hollywood High were either under-achievers or potheads, more attuned to Bugs Bunny cartoons than obscure Oriental theater. This absurdity was not lost on Chris who had to mime his part of the mute propman.

After two *long* hours of quasi-Kabuki acting, Gene chased Chris up the aisle of the auditorium, jabbing him with a sword. Taking a sharp poke in the rear end, the mute propman finally spoke up and screamed one improvised word: "Fuccckkk!!!!"

The dozing audience of teenagers woke up, leaped to their feet, and roared their approval. The auditorium went completely nuts. It was like a prison riot triggered by a renegade convict who dares to thumb his nose at the authorities.

Unfortunately, the school's principal, Dr. Pack, also saw the inspired performance. He was not as thrilled as the kids, and Chris got suspended for a week. When he returned to school, my pal was welcomed back like Cool Hand Luke returning to the chain gang after another amazing escape attempt. His fame on campus certainly trumped mine.

Chris, Gene, and I soon became the "three amigos." We sought out all kinds of dangerous adventures around town: sneaking onto the 20th Century-Fox studio lot to prowl around the sets of *Hello Dolly* and *Planet of the Apes*, exploring the creepy Bronson Caves up in the Hollywood Hills, camping at the beach, and nighttime hikes through Vasquez Rocks, a rugged location used in many TV Westerns and outer space movies. These were some wild times, usually fueled by cheap wine.

The three amigos also discovered a shared love for the American actor John Barrymore, perhaps the greatest thespian of all time. On the surface, he was a dashing and romantic movie star. Deep down, Barrymore had the imagination and versatility of a character actor. He was also the premier "rock star" of his day, a hard partying rebel, something that we admired. On the actor's birthday, I'd throw a raucous drunken party at the Barrymore Suite in the Alexandria Hotel, a decaying old palace in downtown Los Angeles. Those soirees gave me the worst hangovers ever.

Barrymore was also known for pulling outrageous stunts, which Chris and I tried to emulate. On one occasion, we dressed as priests as a ruse to get in to see *The Exorcist*. The movie had just come out, and lines formed around the block for every performance. To bypass the crowds at Grauman's Chinese Theatre, Chris and I went up to the box office and explained that we worked for the New York *Catholic Monitor* and wanted to review the movie; it had become very controversial with the church. We also pointed out "Father Craven's" foot was broken and how difficult it was for him to stand in line. The manager took a look at Chris's "injured" foot, which was actually fine, encased in dozens of white socks to simulate a cast, and ushered us inside, free of charge. He even provided complimentary popcorn and sodas. We couldn't tell if the manager was truly sympathetic or hoping to engender a more favorable review.

As Chris and I watched the movie, we could feel audience members spying on our reactions, especially when the Holy Cross was being desecrated or Linda Blair was screaming blasphemous curses. It took all our strength not to giggle, which garnered even more curious stares. Our biggest fear during that scary movie was that someone in the audience might have a heart attack and we'd be asked to perform the Last Rites. Luckily, nothing that dramatic occurred.

When the show ended, we filed out with the audience who nodded and smiled politely at the "priests." The "holy man" with the broken foot, though, had one more miracle to perform. As we filed past the manager outside the theater, Chris ditched his bogus limp and we broke into a sprint down the street, laughing hysterically at the stunt we had successfully pulled. If there's a special place in hell for priest impersonators, our names are surely on the list.

Even though I was being reckless, there was one big positive: I was finally acting like a normal teenager, experiencing the risky escapades that are a youthful rite of passage. If you survive them, terrific, you've got something to warn your kids about. If you screw up, at least you've got a good excuse, young and dumb. Nobody cuts you much slack when you are older. Maybe that is why so many child actors stumble so frequently as adults; they are forever trying to experience their wild, youthful days that are long gone.

CHAPTER 21

The End Is Here, Now What?

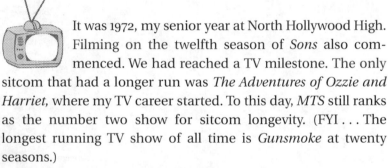It was 1972, my senior year at North Hollywood High. Filming on the twelfth season of *Sons* also commenced. We had reached a TV milestone. The only sitcom that had a longer run was *The Adventures of Ozzie and Harriet*, where my TV career started. To this day, *MTS* still ranks as the number two show for sitcom longevity. (FYI . . . The longest running TV show of all time is *Gunsmoke* at twenty seasons.)

Despite an onslaught of daring new shows like *M*A*S*H*, *Maude*, and *60 Minutes*, our episodes still revolved around lost bicycles, missed dates on prom night, and cookie drives at school. Amazingly, the show was still in the top twenty in the TV Nielsen ratings. With all the turmoil and strife in the real world, perhaps the TV audience needed a retreat from reality. You could always count on *MTS* to transport you into an alternate universe where life was sweet as Uncle Charley's cherry pies.

The producers did make a few halfhearted attempts to reflect the current times. Hair could cover the tops of our ears now, khaki pants didn't always have to be baggy, and we occasionally talked about rock-and-roll music. One episode in the later years even had a story about an English rock star who meets the Douglas family. The producers wanted to hire a real musician and weren't sure who to approach, so they consulted with Stan and me.

Being a huge fan of the Rolling Stones, I suggested Brian Jones, the band's original rhythm guitarist. I thought he dressed cool and that his haircut was impeccable. I was a fan, not necessarily a deep thinker.

Of course, nobody knew that Jones was a flat-out junkie and raging hedonist. It would have been the best inside joke ever if he had accepted the producer's offer and visited our wholesome little universe. As it turned out, Jeremy Clyde from the English pop duo Chad & Jeremy did the episode.

As work on *Sons* plodded along, I began to think about what I might do when the show ended. College was beckoning. My parents advised me to continue my education and pursue an acting career later if I still wanted it.

On the other hand, I was getting solid feedback from our new director, Earl Bellamy, who thought that I had real talent as an actor. He advised me to go straight for a career as an adult performer. I loved the idea, but I also knew that most young performers rarely have careers after they've grown up.

Typecasting was the biggest obstacle to continued success, no matter how talented you were. Once your face is associated with a character from a long-running series, nobody will believe you in a new role. Of course, there were exceptions. Mickey Rooney certainly takes the honors for career longevity. He was MGM's biggest child star in the 1930s and has continued to work throughout his adult life. Elizabeth Taylor made it. So did Roddy McDowall and Jackie Cooper. It seemed like a real crapshoot, though. I knew there were far more casualties than survivors.

One thing was clear in my mind: if I chose a show business career, I wanted to be a character actor, particularly since guys like Jack Nicholson, Gene Hackman, and Warren Oates were changing the face of movies. They were being cast in lead roles, parts that were once the sole domain of classically handsome guys like Rock Hudson or John Wayne. The rise of the character actor in the 1970s gave me a glimmer of hope. I was never going to be the new Robert Redford, but I might have a shot at being the new Dustin Hoffman.

Hard decisions about my future were suddenly upon me at the end of shooting that year: *My Three Sons* was axed. A new CBS programming chief, Fred Silverman, issued an edict: kill every folksy, cornpone comedy that the network aired. *MTS* was being canceled along with *Green Acres*, *Gomer Pyle*, and *The Beverly Hillbillies.*

Ironically, we were still among the top twenty shows in our final season, popular in the Midwest and with older people. Younger TV audiences, the kind that advertisers crave, had abandoned us. It was unlikely that another network would renew the show again, despite our high ratings.

It was time to let it go. All of the original TV sons, Mike, Robbie, and Chip, were no longer living at home. I was the only son left, and I wasn't even a biological offspring, I was the adopted one. It was just Ernie and Dodie holding down the fort. Pretty weak.

On the final day of shooting, there was no great party given by the producers to celebrate our achievement. As in all things with the show, Fred MacMurray set the tone in saying good-bye. He gave me a stiff hug and handshake. That was it. No "thanks, kid, great job" or "here's a gold commemorative wristwatch." That just wasn't his style, and that was okay. MacMurray was full of contradictions, and we just accepted him. He was sweet and gentle, cold and distant, self-effacingly funny but very conservative.

A description of Fred MacMurray wouldn't be complete if I didn't mention his famous frugality. He was perhaps the wealthiest man in Hollywood, which made his tightfisted ways all the more baffling.

One of the funniest stories about MacMurray's penny-pinching ways came from John Stephens, our production manager. MacMurray asked Stephens to round up a few crew members to have a meal with him and then they'd all head to the Pantages Theatre to see a closed-circuit televised heavy-weight fight.

When the dinner bill was delivered, it totaled around fifty dollars, this being early 1960s prices. Rather than pick up the check for the crew members, MacMurray scrutinized the bill and announced the dollar amount that everybody should pay to cover their individual order. Stephens snatched the bill and paid it, pleasing MacMurray immensely. Then, the group piled into the star's station wagon and they were off to the theater.

Once they arrived at the Pantages Theatre, MacMurray realized that the parking lot required one dollar to gain entrance. That was too much money to pay so he scoured the streets for free parking. Eventually, MacMurray gave up the hunt after Stephens pointed out that the prizefight was about to start. MacMurray pulled his wagon into the parking lot, and the attendant asked for the dollar fee. Without a moment's hesitation, the star held out his hand to the group in his car and asked everyone to chip in to help pay for the fee. Everyone obliged.

MacMurray was an enigma, an intensely private man caught up in a high-profile career. He liked being an actor but hated being a celebrity. I could relate, being so uncomfortably famous at public school. In some ways, he was more of a role model than I had realized.

Bottom line: I was very fond of my surrogate "dad." I liked all the members of my TV family and would miss them greatly. After twelve years, some of us were at the end of our careers, while others were on the verge of starting new journeys. I was among the latter.

I was turning eighteen and soon to receive the tens of thousands of dollars from my acting work as a minor. Such a large amount of money was a blessing and a curse at that young age. One way or another, it felt pretty damn exciting.

CHAPTER 22

Free to Be Me

First event on my to-do list was a road trip with buddies. Chris, Gene, Danny Muldorpher, and I piled into my 1969 Camaro and headed north to Sequoia National Forest for a camping trip. Four guys, plus gear, in that little Chevy! I don't know how we managed it, but we did.

I tasted freedom for the first time in my life. No parents, no work schedules, no school! It was magical walking among the giant redwoods, especially after smoking some weed, the new drug of choice among my peers.

I was a sponge, soaking up all the simple joys that I'd been missing out on while I was working. We partied around the campfire, swapped stories about UFOs and Bigfoot sightings, hiked, tried to pick up campground chicks, and slept on the cold ground in sleeping bags. The frozen morning would wake us up, hungover, happy and ever ready for the next adventure.

Once back in Los Angeles, I mulled over my future goals: college or acting. The fall semester at school was a couple of months away, so I thought I'd check out some adult acting classes. I'd had some coaching as a kid with a lady named Lois Auer but never any formal training. One acting teacher's name kept coming up: Jeff Corey. I'd heard that he taught Jack Nicholson, Jane and Peter Fonda, and James Dean. Not too shabby. It seemed like a reasonable place to start, so I enrolled hoping for the best. Instead, I got the worst.

After a few sessions of listening to Corey expound about acting theory, I did a monologue for his class. It was the role of Don Baker from the play, *Butterflies Are Free*. After I finished, Corey proceeded to rip me a new asshole. Apparently, my performance was exemplary of everything that was wrong with "representative acting" as seen on TV. That was a real slur, especially if you subscribed to a Stanislavski "method acting" approach, which Corey did.

Perhaps he was right about my work. I really didn't know. I was just acting by instinct, which had served me pretty well over the years. In any case, there wasn't a tempered, constructive word in Corey's entire, bitter critique. I was barely eighteen, the new kid in class, and got sucker-punched. Perhaps Corey thought he was enlightening his students. Nice for them. He made me feel like I'd farted out loud . . . through my mouth. I looked for another class pronto.

One ironic footnote: A few years later, after I'd studied with more helpful teachers, I starred in a new CBS series called *Sons and Daughters*, and Jeff Corey was hired to direct an episode. When we met on the set, he was suddenly full of praise for my work and said I'd really improved as an actor. Still smarting from his verbal spanking, I replied, "Not in your class I didn't."

My first acting role post–*My Three Sons* was in a USC student film titled *Peege* , a tearjerker about a family visiting their invalid mother in a rest home. It hardly seemed like the next big step in my career. I was hoping for another TV series or a feature film. My agent, Wally Hiller, insisted that I do the film, though. According to Hiller, the film's writer/director, Randal Kleiser, had caught the eye of industry insiders and was destined for big things. My agent was right. Kleiser went on to direct the highest grossing movie musical of all time, *Grease,* among other hits.

Over the years, *Peege* became the highest grossing short subject in film history and won numerous awards, including the prestigious honor of being added to the permanent film collection of the Smithsonian. To this day, over forty years later, I still get a few dollars in residual payments from the small percentage of profits that I was given in the film.

My Three Sons was off the air in prime time now, but that wasn't the end of it. CBS brokered a deal with a syndication distributor to air reruns of the show every day in non–prime time markets all across America.

CBS offered me $50,000 to buy out my share of future payments. That was a whole lot of dough in 1972. I was tempted to take the money and run. If the show flopped in syndication, though, *MTS* would be headed for the vaults, never to be seen again, and I'd be $50,000 poorer. I wasn't hurting for cash at the time, having just received my trust money, so I rejected the CBS offer. It seemed like a good gamble because *MTS* had great ratings its twelfth and final season, meaning the public might not be tired of it yet.

My theory proved to be right. The show was a huge hit in syndication, and I made at least four times the amount that CBS offered. Over the next ten years, that residual money kept me solvent while I figured out what to do with my life.

The next big move I made after *MTS* was leaving my parents' home and getting a residence of my own. I rented the top floor of an old brownstone castle on Detroit Street in Los Angeles, just north of Wilshire Boulevard and the Miracle Mile. The lunatics (Chris, Gene, and me, among others) suddenly had their own playpen. It was nonstop laughing, yelling, pulling pranks, and, of course, pot smoking.

I suppose a disclaimer on the use of drugs should be offered at this time, particularly if any children (including my own) read this book. My friends and I used marijuana to hot-wire our imaginations, not to sedate our senses or get mellow. Getting "high" to us meant getting outside our normal mind-sets. Nonsensical verbal rants were roundly applauded and definitely encouraged. These outbursts occasionally bordered on the poetic, although that was never the intent. The goal was to unleash an unhinged stream of consciousness just to see where it took you. The results were usually hysterically funny, if not for the verbal riffing then for the stupidity exhibited.

Silly characters were sometimes born out of nothing more than a mundane prop that was within reach: a portrait of a Spanish peasant, a bird cage, a vacuum cleaner, anything and everything. Sometimes our word games were coupled with spasmodic dancing or elaborate vaudevillian dance steps, whatever got a laugh. All in all, it was flat out fun. It enabled me to experience a freedom of mind and spirit that I never knew existed. Eventually, this wild improvisational theater was given a name: Beretdom. A friend of mine, Bob Barrios, attended our gatherings and always wore a beret-style hat, thus the inspiration for the name. It had no significant meaning, which in turn gave it great meaning. Beretdom was just a goofy name born out of a wild and crazy theatrical experiment . . . with pot. It seemed to fit, but you probably would have to have been there.

Beretdom was breaking out almost every evening on Detroit Street. These wild improvs were helpful in liberating inhibitions, but I wasn't sure how to apply such madness to the subtleties of acting. It was just too unhinged for scripted material. Eventually, I found another formal acting class taught by Ned Mandarino.

The Mandarino school of acting turned out to be almost as off the wall as Beretdom. Class would start with a lengthy relaxation period sitting in a chair onstage, eyes closed and head drooped forward. Ned would verbally encourage you to imagine things like tiny rodent claws crawling over your skin or enormous pepperoni pizzas hovering above your head. The idea was to open yourself up to a sensory stimulation that would get you up and moving about the stage.

It was funny as hell to watch the actors going from a relaxed stupor to jumping around the stage, crying or laughing hysterically. Mandarino, who was serious as Moses, would bellow random suggestions: "It's raining . . . it's raining puppies . . . it's raining *Hammers!*" The actors would react to whatever Ned threw at them. The process wasn't that much different from Beretdom, except I was paying a few hundred dollars a month for his class.

I dove into all of Mandarino's exercises as sincerely as possible, hoping to become the next Brando or Nicholson or Wally Cox. I really wasn't sure where I was headed. As any young actor will attest, acting classes offer more than just a place to develop your talent; it's where you meet attractive actresses. Dale Bach caught my eye immediately. She looked like Ingrid Bergman, one of my favorite screen stars, and I was smitten.

Frankly, Dale was one of the main reasons I stayed in Ned's class as long as I did. Before I could muster the nerve to ask for a date, though, she dropped out of class, and I quickly lost my enthusiasm for the Mandarino Method. As hard as I tried, I never felt comfortable reciting Shakespeare with "blue bunnies orbiting my head."

CHAPTER 23

The Well-Rounded Performer Sings and Dances

 I finally booked my first major TV job post-*MTS*. I was cast as Linus in a Hallmark Hall of Fame production of the hit stage musical, *You're a Good Man, Charlie Brown*. This job presented a real performance challenge: I would have to sing and dance. All of those lessons from Eddie Gay and Madame Etienne were about to pay off. I even had a big solo number, "My Blanket and Me." My mom, needless to say, was ecstatic. Her dream had come true. I was finally going to be a well-rounded entertainer.

I knew my tap time-steps and could hold a melody, but, honestly, this new job terrified me. I was never going to be Gene Kelly, no matter what my mother said. I wasn't even close to wearing Gene Autry's boots, for that matter. American musical theater didn't consume me the way it consumed a lot of other actors. My show tune repertoire was so impoverished that I resorted to singing *Song of the South*'s "Zip-a-Dee-Doo-Dah" at my audition. That was about as deep as my song library went—Disney movies. Nonetheless, the producers saw me as Linus, and I was hired.

Poseur paranoia immediately kicked in; I was certain that the producers had overestimated my abilities. Singing like Uncle Remus is one thing, but doing their show's complex four-part harmonies was quite another. I'd also have to measure up to the other cast members that were cherry picked for their excellence from all the other *Charlie Brown* productions around the country.

Making matters even more stressful, the producers were tough theater veterans such as the director Joseph Hardy and Patricia Birch. She was the brilliant choreographer who went on to design the dances in the original production of *Grease* on Broadway. I feared I'd be the one out-of-tune violin in this orchestra of virtuosos. I had two weeks before rehearsals started, and I dropped everything to prepare.

For the next fourteen days, I spent every spare moment working with a dance teacher, Dean Barlow (an Emmy winner for work with Paula Abdul), and a singing coach, Marie Golden, whose specialty was whipping run-of-the-mill actors into instant singers. During that time I became a tap-dancing, scale-singing maniac trying to whip myself into credible shape.

As rehearsals for *Charlie Brown* commenced, I learned that I was as competent as the other actors. What I lacked in song-and-dance excellence, I made up for in television acting experience. That was a relief.

Fortunately, Pat Birch could tailor her choreography to each performer's ability. On the high end was Bill Hinnant, the original Snoopy off-Broadway. Hinnant was a really good singer and dancer, so Birch designed some pretty elaborate moves for him. I was on the low end of competence, and Birch, gratefully, kept my dance steps simple but no less creative. After a couple of weeks of rehearsals, we were ready for showtime.

We moved to the NBC studios in Burbank to tape the musical. While I was there, I dropped in on my old best buddy, Fred De Cordova, who was on the lot producing Johnny Canson's *The Tonight Show*.

I was greeted with hugs, kisses, and the usual sarcastic repartee. He even accompanied me back to our soundstage to watch our dress rehearsal. My stock rose immensely when the *Charlie Brown* producers saw me with my important pal. It was a huge publicity boost if De Cordova allowed you on his program to promote your project. Salivating at the prospect, the producers approached us and inquired about Charles Schulz, Charlie Brown's creator, going on *The Tonight Show*. It would be Schulz's first televised interview ever, quite a coup. De Cordova jumped at the opportunity and granted their request. Without missing a beat, he added one caveat: "Barry must be on the show, too."

My jaw dropped at De Cordova's request. I had dreamed of being on *The Tonight Show* with Carson. The producers exchanged furtive looks and nodded gamely, mumbling what a great idea that was. I could see they weren't thrilled, but the deal was sealed with a handshake.

What actually transpired on my *Tonight Show* appearance was far from what I'd hoped for. I envisioned Schulz and I sitting across from Johnny, trading barbs, swapping clever anecdotes, and sipping drinks from those *Tonight Show* mugs. It turned out that my loyal *Charlie Brown* producers had a subsequent talk with De Cordova and insisted that only Schulz should converse with Carson. They suggested that a few cast members, including me, could sing a song from the show about Charlie Brown's kite. De Cordova agreed to the compromise, and that's the way it went down. Schulz sat alone with Carson, blabbing on like Geppetto the puppet master, and we trotted out to sing like his little marionettes.

After we taped the musical, the entire cast was flown to New York to record the show's songs for an album. Working in a professional recording studio in the heart of Manhattan was a great new experience.

It also whetted my appetite for living there someday and working on the Broadway stage, just like my idol, John Barrymore. I tracked down my acting hero's Greenwich Village apartment, the Alchemist's Corner, where his Hamlet was born. I also made a point to have my first legal drink at the Algonquin Hotel, one of Barrymore's last residences and the location of the infamous Round Table Meetings in the 1920s. It was a real kick to sip my whiskey in the smoky, oak-paneled bar and imagine the ghostly voices of Barrymore, Dorothy Parker, George S. Kaufman, Robert Benchley, Noel Coward, and all the other brilliant minds who met up there to match wits.

On the last night of my trip, I had one more highlight: participating in a George McGovern for President rally held at the Palace Theatre. Being a TV celebrity, and the youngest voter onstage, I was given a prime spot on the dais. I took advantage of my position to shake hands with one of my modern acting idols, Gene Wilder, and he couldn't have been nicer. It was a great way to finish up an inspiring trip to the Big Apple.

CHAPTER 24

Moving to the Bunker

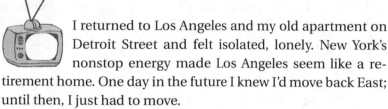 I returned to Los Angeles and my old apartment on Detroit Street and felt isolated, lonely. New York's nonstop energy made Los Angeles seem like a retirement home. One day in the future I knew I'd move back East; until then, I just had to move.

I went apartment hunting in the hills of Studio City and, by dumb luck, drove past a For Rent sign at 4050 Fairway Avenue. I wandered up a stairway into a jungle paradise of palms, exotic flowers, and huge sprawling ferns. The complex had four terraced levels with an apartment on each one, totally unique residences made of wood, glass, and cinder block. I was wowed. I continued to the top level where the proprietors, Dick and Julie Weaver, lived in an amazing two-story ultramodern home.

It turns out Dick was an architect and built the complex himself. He designed each unit to be a state-of-the-art, all-electric residence, a concept popularized by the Monsanto House of the Future at Disneyland. This seemed like the perfect new headquarters for my Beret Brothers: an apartment in Fantasyland.

I wasted no time moving into my new residence. My pals soon dubbed the place the Bunker, for its gray cinder block walls and clubhouse vibe. It was a pot-smoking free zone and open 24/7.

I began to worry about the landlords' reaction to our loud

improvised routines and hysterical laughter, not to mention the plumes of smoke wafting out the windows. They never complained, though. It turned out the Weavers were already immune to such insanity because a psychologist specializing in Primal Scream therapy worked right next door.

I found out about the doctor's practice and the blood-curdling cries of his patients the first day I moved in. I was unpacking boxes, setting up shop, when I heard desperate, agonized screams that went on and on. I didn't have a phone installed, so I ran to the landlords' house and pounded on their door.

Dick Weaver answered, and I said, "I just heard somebody screaming. I think somebody is being murdered next door."

He laughed and said, "It's just Doctor Otto with a patient."

"Doctor Otto? You're sure it's not Doctor Mengele, the Nazi? I've never heard such screaming."

"It's Primal Scream therapy," Weaver replied. "Sometimes his patients are reliving their childbirths."

Ouch.

The Weavers must have thought the noise from my apartment was like a whisper compared to the agonized yelling next door. It was a very freewheeling, tolerant time. The early 1970s was the height of hedonism: nudist camps, disco decadence, and Primal Scream therapy.

CHAPTER 25

Work After *My Three Sons*

 It had been awhile since my last acting job, so I started to seriously think about going to college. I enrolled in UCLA and, true to Murphy's Law, was offered guest star roles on three different TV shows. They were all dramatic in tone, a real departure from Ernie Douglas. I hated the idea of abandoning school, but the roles were very tempting. I put my higher education on hold.

The first role was in a series titled *Ironside* starring Raymond Burr as a wheelchair-bound detective. I played an embittered teenage paraplegic who was also in a wheelchair. Mr. Burr graciously offered me personal instructions on maneuvering my wheelchair. He also gave me a few sly winks and a pat on my bottom, which I took as a sign that I was doing a good job. Silly me. I was told later that he liked young men and, if the rumor was true, owned an island off Tahiti that was full of boys in loincloths.

The next show I did was *Room 222* created by Gene Reynolds, the director who brought me onto *My Three Sons*. I played a political radical, a flat-out Lenin-loving communist, in fact. My Uncle Bernard, a lifelong member of the Communist Party, couldn't have been more pleased about my new role.

The last in the trio of parts was on *The Streets of San Francisco*. I played a runaway teen fleeing from abusive parents.

Larry Wilcox played my older brother. He became famous a few years later as Erik Estrada's partner on the TV series, *CHiPS*. One of the real thrills of this project was working with a screen legend, Karl Malden.

Malden was a masterful actor and performed brilliantly in such great movies as *A Streetcar Named Desire, On the Waterfront,* and *Nevada Smith.* I asked for his advice on a scene where I had to break down and cry. He eagerly obliged and coached me through a couple of "sense memory exercises," which helped me tap into my emotions. I was able to bring those feelings into the scene where I confront my evil parents, and, sure enough, the tears flowed. It was a great lesson shared by a great actor.

I had another memorable moment on *The Streets of San Francisco.* Actually, it was more like a near-death mishap.

It was written in the script that my character was supposed to drive a 1950s Ford pickup. Before shooting commenced, I told the producers to find a truck that had an automatic transmission because I didn't know how to drive a stick shift. They assured me that they would take care of it. Never trust a producer.

When I arrived on the set in San Francisco, the first thing I did was ask to see the truck. An assistant director pointed to an old, battered Ford parked on a steep incline. He said, "I think that old hunk of junk is it."

Hunk of junk was being kind. Every section of the truck—the doors, the hood, the front panels—was dented and painted different colors. Even the windshield was cracked.

"No way that's an automatic," I grumbled as I walked over to the multicolored wreck.

I peered into the truck's cab and saw three pedals: gas, brake, clutch . . . a manual transmission. The gearshift handle was located on the steering column instead of on the floor and was jerry-rigged with rubber bands to provide some kind of tension.

A burly teamster sidled alongside of me and said, "Ya gotta

use both of yer hands to move the shifter when ya wanna switch gears. She's a bitch."

"You mean I'll have to let go of the steering wheel while the truck is moving to change gears?" I asked.

"Uh-huh. It's a bitch," the teamster replied with a heavy sigh.

I tracked down the assistant director. I pointed to my *bitch* and said, "The truck was supposed be an automatic. I told the producers *not* to get a stick shift because I don't know how to drive one!"

Assistant directors are easily the most stressed people on every film set, responsible for keeping the expensive shooting schedules on track. His eyes glazed over as he groped for an answer. "I'd better get someone to teach you," he muttered. "Your scene is up in about thirty minutes."

Moments later, I was sitting behind the Ford's oversized steering wheel, waving away the torn ceiling liner tickling the top of my head. A stunt man sat next to me in the passenger seat, having volunteered to be my tutor.

As anyone who's ever driven a manual transmission knows, learning takes time and practice. I had neither. We lurched and stalled, lurched and stalled, over and over as my feet tap-danced between the clutch, the brake, and the accelerator pedals. After thirty minutes of getting nowhere, literally, the assistant director said it was time to shoot the scene.

"You think I'm ready to do this?" I asked the stunt man.

His face clouded with concern. Then he mustered up a weak smile and said, "Sure, go for it." He quickly hopped out of the car before I could call him a liar.

Next thing I know, I'm sitting in my idling Ford at the top of a hill and San Francisco is sprawling out below me. My palms went from clammy to sweaty as I clutched the giant steering wheel. I peered over the Ford's bulbous hood, and I couldn't even see the street in front of me, that's how steep the descent was. The director's voice crackled through a walkie-talkie lying on the passenger seat: "Okay, Barry, action!"

With the clutch depressed, I used both hands to yank on the steering column shifter and pull it up into first gear. Then with a silent prayer, or perhaps it was a curse, I gave it a little gas and slowly released the clutch pedal. The Ford inched forward and kept rolling. It looked like I was going to drive right off a cliff until the truck's nose dipped downward. At last, I saw a long black ribbon of road dropping before me. It was like sitting in the front seat of a roller coaster and staring down at the first nauseating drop.

The truck picked up speed, and I put a death grip on the steering wheel. No way was I going to take my hands off that goddamn wheel and monkey around with that funky column shifter. I came up with my own plan: depress the clutch to the floorboard, stay in neutral, and "ride the brake" to the bottom.

Of course, the weight of the truck and the laws of gravity had something to say about my plan. Despite my constant braking, the old Ford was going faster and faster. It began to rattle like an overloaded washing machine with me inside hanging on.

About midway down the slope, I saw the camera crew on the sidewalk filming my descent. I raced past them in a blur and prayed they got the shot. If there was a technical malfunction, I'd have to go back to the top of the hill and do it again. The walkie-talkie next to me came alive again, and the director's voice sputtered: "That's a print! Let's move on." Those were sweet words to hear, except that I was still barreling downhill at top speed.

The only thing on my mind was stopping that old Ford before it rattled to pieces. Looming ahead was an intersection with a red light. I pressed harder on the brake pedal, hoping for a safe conclusion to my crazy ride. No such luck. The pedal melted to the floorboard, a sign that the master cylinder had failed. "No brakes!" I yelled to nobody in particular.

I arrived at the red light doing at least forty miles per hour and swerved through the cross traffic, barely missing a couple of cars. Once on the other side of the intersection, the road started to ascend. The runaway truck eventually slowed enough for me to turn it perpendicular to the hill and come to a stop. I'd made it out alive. Barely.

Back in Los Angeles, I got a couple more jobs notable for the people involved. The first was an Alan King special where Ron Howard, Opie from *The Andy Griffith Show,* and I did a sketch. This was before his directing career took off and he was still acting. I was to play the Teenager from Today and Ron was playing the Teenager from Yesterday. Our characters were going to meet and compare notes about our lives.

I knew Ron only as an acquaintance, from a few showbiz social functions, and he seemed like a nice guy. We weren't overly friendly, though, and I sensed a competitiveness. We were both successful child actors, occasionally vying for the same roles. This rivalry surfaced during the sketch.

On Ron's first line of dialogue, he took a big step upstage so that my face was pointing away from the camera. This is called "upstaging" another actor. It's a cheap theatrical trick and allows the perpetrator to gain undue focus in the scene. I was no rube and saw what was happening. I countered his upstage movement by stepping upstage on my next line.

That's the way it went through the whole two-page scene. Ron would step back while speaking and then I would step back while responding. By the end of the scene we had moved six feet away from our marks and were standing in the dark, far from where the lights were focused or the camera could film us.

The director finally stepped in and ordered us to stay put, and that ended the gamesmanship. I never saw or worked with Ron again. Given his sterling reputation for directing actors, though, I'm sure he'd never allow an actor to get away with such shenanigans. Chalk it up to youth.

The other job I landed was in a short-lived sitcom, *Thicker Than Water.* The best part of this gig was working with Julie Harris, the revered Broadway actress and James Dean's costar in

East of Eden. She was a consummate professional, a fact under-scored by a prank that went terribly wrong.

It was two in the afternoon, the end of our lunch hour, and the actors, writers, and producers convened in a conference room to read the script. There was just one problem: the show's star, Ms. Harris, was absent.

The director, Jerry Paris, was a notorious prankster and thought it would be funny if we started the reading without her, just to see her reaction once she joined us. There was no malice or lesson intended. He thought she'd break up laughing once the joke was revealed. Boy, was he wrong.

Around 2:06, Ms. Harris rushed into the room. Seeing us reading from the script, she stopped dead in her tracks and gasped. With her head bowed, she quietly took her place at the head of the table, her pale freckled face flushing red. Pressing on with the gag, Paris frowned at her and whispered, "We decided to start without you, Julie. We're on a tight schedule."

Ms. Harris then burst into tears. She looked to the group and sobbed, "I'm so very sorry. I didn't mean to make everyone wait for me. I truly apologize . . ."

Seeing his star traumatized, Paris backpedaled. "Julie, Julie, Julie! It was just a joke. It was my idea. I never dreamed you'd get so upset."

Hearing that, her sobbing stopped. Ms. Harris focused like a marksman on Paris, her jaw clenched. You could hear a sneeze from the next room it was so quiet. We all held our breath wait-ing for her to unload.

Finally, she said in a controlled tremble, "I'm sorry that I ar-rived late. I was caught in a wardrobe fitting. If it wouldn't be too much trouble for everyone, could we start from the beginning?"

Ever the pro, she put the work ahead of lashing back at Paris, and we started over. The mood wasn't exactly primed for a comedy.

Another odd, prophetic moment happened on this show with Richard Long, another series regular and a well-established

TV star. We were standing together backstage about to make our entrance before a live studio audience. Long discreetly pulled a small vile from his pocket, extracted a few tiny white pills, amphetamines I guessed, and gobbled them down.

The actor glanced over at me with a wink and a rascal smile. "Time to be *funny*," he said.

Richard Long died of a heart attack about a year later at the age of forty-seven. The white pills were most likely nitroglycerine.

CHAPTER 26

Myrna

 My recent flurry of jobs culminated with an ABC Suspense Movie of the Week, *The Elevator*. It led to a cherished memory with one of my legendary costars.

It was after midnight when I finished work. I'd been "trapped" in a real elevator in a Los Angeles skyscraper with Roddy McDowall, Teresa Wright, Craig Stevens, and Myrna Loy. Good company when you're pretending to be stuck in an airless box for hours at a time.

Now that I was released, I hurried to my dressing room to change clothes and, more importantly, use the bathroom. I know, that's more information than you wanted to hear. It's a salient point, though, because my delay in the john had an unexpected ripple effect. By the time I'd run downstairs and hit the street, I'd missed the company's shuttle van to a city parking lot where I'd left my car that morning. Worse yet, I was locked out of the building that we were working in, stranded in L.A.'s seedy skid row. I began cursing aloud just as a Cadillac limo pulled up to the curb.

The vehicle's blacked-out window descended and Myrna Loy peered out from the rear compartment. She was a bona fide movie star, and the studio, rightfully so, provided her with a limo. I was never more grateful to see a friendly face.

"Are you okay?" she asked.

"The studio van going to my parking lot left without me, and I can't get back in the building to get help," I said. "I'm stuck."

"Oh!" she exclaimed with a laugh. "Never keep a teamster driver waiting, that's rule number one!" She flung open the limo's door. "We'll take you to your car. Hop in."

I didn't hesitate to accept her offer. Moments before, I was angry about missing my ride in the back of a cramped company van. Now, I was traveling in style with one of the most beautiful, elegant, and revered screen legends in film history.

I was twenty-one at the time and had seen many of Myrna's classic films: *Too Hot to Handle, Manhattan Melodrama,* and *Test Pilot,* all starring opposite Clark Gable; *The Bachelor and the Bobby-Soxer* with Cary Grant; and the Academy Award–winning film *The Best Years of Our Lives.* My favorite movie, though, was *The Thin Man* and its numerous sequels.

Myrna played Nora Charles, the sexy, sassy private eye who cracked baffling crimes with the help of her husband Nick (William Powell) and their amazingly intelligent dog, Asta. I liked the whole concept: husband and wife as private eyes, spiffy penthouse living, and a dog that was smarter than the crooks they busted. The movie series made Myrna a model of style, independence, and sophistication.

As our limo glided along, Myrna poured us red wine in tall delicate crystal glasses. As I sipped my cabernet, I started feeling pretty sophisticated myself, like a junior Nick Charles.

We'd been working together for a week, but there hadn't been an opportunity to talk to her about her illustrious career. Now that we were alone, I wanted to ask something halfway intelligent. From what I'd seen of her on film, she didn't suffer fools.

"So . . . what was Asta like?" I blurted out. The little voice in my head yelled: *"Jesus Christ! A dog?! How lame! You should have asked about Gable or Fredric March. What an idiot!"*

Myrna chuckled and said, "Everybody always wants to know about Asta. He was a terrier, you know, quite hyper. The little bastard bit me once, too."

I laughed. The sophisticated lady said *bastard,* which caught me off guard.

"Wasn't Asta also in *Bringing Up Baby* with Cary Grant?" I asked, even though I already knew the answer was *yes.* I just wanted to keep the ball rolling.

"Practically stole the movie," she replied. "The studio wasn't going to fire that damn dog. He was getting more fan mail than me." Myrna sipped her wine and shook her head with a sigh.

"Yeah, wire-haired terriers." That was my brilliant retort, real numbskull speak. I took another stab at witty repartee and said, "I worked with a dog on *My Three Sons.* He was kind of dumb but nice."

Myrna stared out her rear window without a reaction. Guess she never watched TV. That medium was probably beneath her refined sensibility. She was probably an opera buff or a patron of the ballet. I downed the last drop of my wine and wanted more but refrained from asking. It might appear uncouth and all.

Myrna must have sensed my thirst because she reached for the bottle and poured me another full glass. "I liked to watch *Bonanza.* That was kind of like *My Three Sons* only with horses," she said.

"Yeah, you're right. I never realized that," I replied. Apparently she did watch TV, and Westerns, too!

We rode in silence, sipping our wine. I tried to rekindle the conversation and said, "I'm thinking about going to New York."

"Why?" she murmured, casually engaged by my small talk.

"That's what Roddy (McDowall) said he did when he was my age. I want to be a better actor and, hopefully, not get stereotyped."

Myrna looked at me as if for the very first time. "I had that problem in the beginning of my career. For some reason, I got typecast as an Asian," she said with a chuckle.

"Asian?" I replied. I tried to picture her playing a native of the Far East . . . and couldn't. She was just Nora Charles to me.

"For the first five years in my career I played Burmese, Chinese, Japanese, South Seas, whatever. The makeup people said it had something to do with the structure around my eyes. Imagine, a redhead from Montana being cast as an Oriental vamp?!"

"You're from Montana? Wow. No wonder you like Westerns," I said. I began to see Myrna in a new light. "How did you break out of playing Asians?"

"First you've got to *break in*, which is what those roles did for me. After you're *in*, then you can think about *breaking out*. Be patient, and it will happen if you're good, which I was. You are, too."

"Thanks," I said, savoring the compliment from such a talented and worldly person. Despite our big age difference, she was still attractive, and I had a sudden urge to kiss her. This desire caught me by surprise. I wasn't really romantically inclined. It felt more like a cocky whim to demonstrate my worldliness. Blame it on two tall glasses of wine in a short period of time.

At last, the limo pulled into the parking lot and stopped next to my car. Myrna made direct eye contact, making sure she had my full attention, and said, "You know, I've been playing so-called sophisticated women for over thirty years now, a lifetime. Not long ago, somebody suggested me for the role of the Chinese empress in the film, *55 Days at Peking*, and do you know what the producer said: "You mean Nora Charles?! She couldn't possibly pull off playing an Asian!" Myrna laughed, tickled by the memory. "People make assumptions. They see what they want to see."

I gazed back at her. Her famous, up-turned nose was still pretty sexy. I thought, *Go ahead, give her a kiss! It's now or never!*

Myrna put her hand on my cheek and said, "You're so young. You can go anywhere, be anybody you want to be. Do what your heart tells you, Barry."

Those were just the words I needed to hear. I leaned over and kissed her on the cheek. As my lips pulled away, my face was close to hers. I said, "Well, then . . . thanks for the ride." It wasn't the smooth, seductive overture that I'd hoped for. I lingered in her space a bit too long, too, waiting for a follow-up line that never came. Suave William Powell was twirling in his grave.

Myrna seemed amused by my geeky advance. "You're welcome," she said with a chuckle. Our eyes were still locked on each other. I wasn't sure where things would go next and then . . .

The limo's rear door popped open. The driver peered inside at us, which really put a damper on my romantic moment.

"I'll see you tomorrow, my dear," Myrna said, gently dismissing her "tipsy suitor," just like I'd seen her do in a dozen of her movies.

After a final grateful nod, I slid out of the car before my adrenaline-pumping brain gave me a heart attack.

I watched her limo driving away and smiled. *I just kissed Nora Charles.*

CHAPTER 27

Meanwhile, Back Home at the Ranch

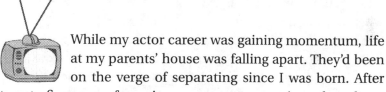 While my actor career was gaining momentum, life at my parents' house was falling apart. They'd been on the verge of separating since I was born. After twenty-five years of marriage, my mom was serious about leaving my dad. He was in his late fifties and was done living up to the high expectations of his youth. No more halfhearted attempts at writing the Great American Novel or returning to college to get a degree in psychology or law. Working as a salesman at Charles Furniture in Watts would be the pinnacle of his professional life. It was a depressing revelation, but an honest one. There was little point in torturing himself anymore about his shortcomings. My dad hoped that my mom would accept this. She didn't.

My mom felt betrayed by my dad's failure to launch. She had bought a first-class ticket for a ride on the Spruce Goose, only to learn that the amazing plane was never going to fly. She wanted her money back, and then some. Her growing dissatisfaction about life wasn't restricted to my dad; I was suddenly in her crosshairs.

I was a young adult now, eager to take control of my future, whether it was in show business or not. I no longer needed or desired my mother's participation in my career. Blame it on a young man's ego or vanity. One way or the other, my declaration of independence didn't sit well with her. She felt abandoned. In her eyes, I wasn't showing enough gratitude for her efforts that built my career. She played the motherly "guilt card," and that stung.

Granted, I was a young man, and no doubt self-absorbed, but I tried to show my appreciation as best I could. I soon realized, though, that no amount of hugs and kisses, applause or words of thanks could fix her low self-esteem or fill the echoing void in her life. She had no real education, no professional life, not even a hobby. All that my mom had was a failed marriage and another son who was leaving the nest. It was pretty overwhelming, for her and me.

I came around the house as much as possible, hoping to mediate a truce between my parents. That was a dangerous mission. Their anger seemed as complex as the war between the Jews and Palestinians.

Despite my best efforts, their "cold war" would occasionally break out into physical hostilities. Once, my mom cracked a bust of Albert Einstein over my dad's head. That was quite an ironic comment considering my father's supposed genius status.

Unfortunately, my younger siblings, Bill and Michelle, were still living at home and had to witness the ugliness. I'd get them out of the house as much as possible, to the movies or the zoo, but it was never enough. I wished I could have done more. Parents are like superpowers in their children's world. There's not much that Poland can do to stop a war between Russia and the United States.

CHAPTER 28

Life Beyond the Camera

My financial independence was a blessing in two ways. I could afford an apartment, allowing me to escape the problems at home, and it funded my youthful adventures. Gene and I started to venture onto the Hollywood club scene looking for fun and chicks. One of our newest discoveries was Rodney Bingenheimer's English disco on the Sunset Strip, a place where I got into the only fistfight of my life.

Rodney's was a hangout for the burgeoning glam-rock scene in the early 1970s. Boys and girls would camp it up wearing makeup, sequined halter tops, and enormous platform shoes. The fashion was modeled after David Bowie's Ziggy Stardust unisex character. I wasn't keen on eyeliner, sequins, or shirts exposing my belly button. I was very pleased about platform boots, though. They had soles that were three inches thick or more, depending on how high you wanted to go. I opted for the max since I was height challenged at five foot five. These new elevator shoes were the greatest development in footwear since Beatle boots, unless you got into a scuffle.

My brawl began innocently enough. I noticed John Barrymore Jr. (of all people) entering the club. Being a huge fan of his father, I pointed Junior out to my wingman, Gene. A teenage

Glam Boy in skin-tight pants, skimpy T-shirt, and platform shoes overheard me and butted in.

"That's not John Barrymore Junior!" said Glam Boy. His words were slurred, probably from the quaalude he'd taken.

"Hell, yes! I've seen pictures of him. That is Barrymore, Junior," I insisted. I was an authority on all things Barrymore. I was also drunk from slugging vodka from my flask.

The gauntlet had been thrown down. A nose-to-nose stare-down ensued, like boxers before a championship fight. I was smoking a cigarette for added tough-guy effect. When I exhaled, I made sure a little extra smoke went into Glam Boy's face.

"Don't blow smoke in my face," he growled.

I did it again. The vodka made me do it.

Suddenly, I had a moment of fuzzy clarity through the mix of booze and raging testosterone: I really didn't want a fight. Hoping to *ignore* my opponent away, I looked at Gene who was standing next to me. Bad move. Glam Boy's fist clobbered me on the side of the face. It was a sucker punch that I deserved, for looking away if nothing else.

I reeled backward, skidding on the heels of my three-inch platform shoes. It was an amazing feat of skill to stay upright for as long as I did. My luck ended when my ass hit a table, and I flipped over it like Festus in Miss Kitty's saloon.

In an instant, I wobbled back up onto my platform shoes with the crowd screaming and cheering as if in an echo chamber. My new brown suede jacket was soaked in Tequila sunrises. Now I was really pissed. I zeroed in on Glam Boy who had retreated onto the crowded, swirling dance floor. Elton John's song, "Saturday Night's Alright for Fighting," started to blare over the club's sound system. I took my cue and I charged like a bull out for blood.

I caught up to my assailant right under the flashing mirrored disco ball and threw my best wild punch. Glam Boy ducked, and I accidentally punched some innocent schnook dancing the

Bump with his girlfriend. The poor unsuspecting kid went tumbling, and Glam Boy ran from the dance floor.

Before I could give chase, a human baboon leaped onto my back, and I fell to the ground under his weight. It may have been an ally of Glam Boy or a pal of the guy I'd punched or just some crazy ape leaping into the fray for the fun of it. One way or the other, the guy pinned my shoulders to the floor with his knees and proceeded to tenderize my face with his fists. Amazingly, I didn't feel a thing. My head absorbed the blows like a hollow coconut.

Somehow I pushed the ape off of me and crawled across the dance floor on all fours, weaving between the flailing, kicking legs.

I reached a wall and got to my feet. Out on the dance floor, everyone was throwing punches. It was a real barroom brawl. Gene ran up to me, unscathed, not a hair mussed.

"Where the hell were you?" I asked. "Why didn't you help?"

"I couldn't find you! The place went nuts!" he said. "Let's get out of here!"

Duh!

Seconds later, Gene and I exited the club and were out on Sunset Boulevard, happy to have escaped the melee with teeth intact. As we walked to my parked car, I heard a voice yell at us.

"Hey! Come back here!" Glam Boy had just come out of the club with a posse of buddies sporting halter tops and orange hair. "You're a dead man, asshole!"

The mob sprinted toward us, and the race to my car was on.

Gene and I were running about twenty feet in front of a herd of galloping glam boys. Thank god they were all wearing tall platform shoes, too, or they would have caught us easily.

I arrived at the driver's door of my Camaro, unlocked it, and leaped inside. I was safe, but not Gene. He was still outside the car, pounding on the passenger-side window and yanking on his locked door handle. There was no such thing as automatic door locks in those days. I had to reach over and unlock it manually. This was eating up precious seconds as the glam boys were closing in for the kill. Gene screamed, *"Barry! Hurry! Open the dooorr!"*

I finally flicked the lock, and Gene dove inside, relocking the door with mind-boggling speed. I fired up the Camaro's engine and stomped on the car's accelerator just as the spitting, cursing herd arrived. Unfortunately, we couldn't escape fast enough to avoid a few shoe kicks that left some serious dents in my car's rear end.

I went to an auto body shop a few days later to get a quote on the cost of repairing my Camaro. When the body shop man asked what happened, I lied. I said that baldheaded thugs wielding baseball bats did the damage, not hard-kicking glam boys wearing massive sequined platform shoes.

Hollywood clubs seemed a bit too dangerous, so I looked to the great outdoors for my next adventure, and nearly got killed there, too.

My friend, Brad Huber, and I hatched a plan to shoot the rapids of the Kern River. Of course, we had no experience whatsoever in river rafting. It just seemed like a fun, wild thing to do. I was in the Iron John stage of my young manhood, a time of testing my macho, where every crazy adventure had to have a brush with death. Dumb, but necessary, I guess.

We borrowed a sturdy rubber raft from a friend and set off at four in the morning for the river, accompanied by my new girlfriend, Tess. As daylight broke, we drove down a narrow pass in the Sierra Nevada mountains and saw the Kern River casually snaking its way alongside the road. It gave me butterflies, especially since we had just passed a roadside billboard that said: BE CAREFUL AT THE RIVER. FIVE PEOPLE HAVE LOST THEIR LIVES THIS YEAR! It was only March, too, pretty early in the year for such a high casualty rate. We joked about how the number *five* on the sign was interchangeable, like the squares used on old baseball scoreboards. Whoever managed the billboard wasn't stupid; he knew that number needed changing on a regular basis.

I drove until we found a calm pond in the river where we could launch our rubber raft. The plan was for Tess to drive my car to a riverside campground we had passed; Brad and I would follow the river's course, and we'd all meet up there.

I inflated our spongy yellow vessel with a foot pump and then we shoved off from the riverbank. The lazy river gently guided us away just like Lewis and Clark. Our confidence was high, cocky, in fact. So cocky that we kept our wallets in our pockets and neglected to put on our puffy orange life preservers. This is called tempting fate. We were asking for it.

The first run of whitewater loomed ahead. I was upfront in the raft using my paddle to chart a course between the river rocks; Brad was seated behind me and kept his paddle in the water like a rudder. We were copying the method we'd seen Huck Finn and Tom Sawyer employ on the old *Mickey Mouse Club* show. Not exactly the best tutorial in river rafting, but it worked.

Our tiny raft accelerated, bobbed, and weaved in the surging current as we whooped and yelled from the adrenaline rush. Then . . . we entered another calm patch of water in the river.

"Whooaaa! We did it!" I said.

The raft took on a little chilly water. Other than that, we figured we could handle this river, nothing to it. Then I noticed something odd about our boat.

"Hey, Brad, am I crazy or is our raft getting smaller?" I asked.

Brad squeezed the rubber tubing. "Feels like it's lost a little air. Maybe we hit a submerged rock."

"Or it had a hole to begin with," I said. "Let's head to shore and check it out."

We aimed our raft toward riverbank and paddled hard. The nose of our craft suddenly had a mind of its own and turned back downstream. Another set of rapids downstream was pulling us away from shore and back into the middle of the

river. We picked up speed, and before you could yell *Help!* we
were on another roller-coaster ride.

Forget paddling anymore, we were at the mercy and whims
of the Kern, going whichever way she wanted to toss us. Our raft
bounced high and low. Large rocks appeared midstream and
then disappeared under the swirling water. Waterspouts danced
in the air, splashing our faces with frigid water. The river
seemed to be in a rage, determined to teach a couple of teenage
goofballs a lesson. We raced around a bend in the river, and
the turbulent water calmed back down, again, into another
large open pool.

"Holy shit! Look how small our raft is!" I said. When we began
our journey, the rubber boat was fully inflated, firm and oval
shaped. Now it looked like we were sitting in a flaccid rubber
donut.

We glided through the pond and saw a campground come
into view; it was the designated meeting place with Tess. She
was standing on a rock that jutted out into the river, waving her
arms wildly, urging us to paddle to shore. Once again, the river
had other plans for us.

The current accelerated and pulled our raft back into the
middle of the river. We were now heading for a large rock that
divided the rushing water into two streams. Beyond the rock
was a ten-foot drop, a roaring waterfall. Beyond that, assuming
we'd survive the fall, was more churning whitewater running
through a narrow canyon, bigger and faster than anything we'd
seen yet.

The front of the raft crashed into the big rock and the back
end of our little boat swung around with the rushing current. The raft tipped downward, teetering at the top of the
falls, and Brad was ejected from his seat, thrown into the
waterfall.

Then my end of the raft took the plunge; I grabbed the rubber
dingy with one hand, a paddle with my other. For a brief exhilarating moment I was flying in midair.

The "fun" ended as I splashed down into the water with a painful crash. Somehow I held on to the raft and paddle, kept my head above water, and was swept away. Brad was nowhere to be seen. He was somewhere under the waves.

Clinging to my raft, I took whatever the river threw at me. First obstacle: a massive jagged block of granite. I braced for impact, keeping my squishy raft in front of me. Just as I'd hoped, the rubber boat bounced off the rock, and I avoided a crushing blow. That was the good news. The bad news: I ricocheted back into the raging current and the whirlpools.

I was fully engulfed in the river's fury, but thanks to that beautiful, flimsy raft I was able to keep my head above the rapids.

Brad was not so lucky. I scanned the whitewater but didn't see him anywhere. I feared he fell victim to the infamous Kern whirlpools. If you get sucked into one of those, it's impossible to escape, and you are certain to drown.

Suddenly, a pair of flailing arms broke through the waves ahead of me, and Brad's sopping wet head emerged. Panic was in his eyes as he gasped for air and then was pulled under again. That odd, terrifying picture of my friend repeated itself a few more times, but there was nothing I could do to help him. The river was our master. I was just happy to know he was still alive.

As quickly as the river raged it settled down, and I floated into a calm pool. I looked around for Brad, and he was behind me now with his head above water and dog-paddling to the shore. Tess had been running along the riverbank and was there to greet us when we crawled up onto a sandy beach.

Exhausted and terrified, my buddy and I lay on the river's shore and saw the beating the Kern had given us: torn pants, cuts, scrapes, and instant bruises. There was nothing to do but laugh; we had survived. We had tempted the river god and she took pity on our stupidity. We were lucky.

There was one odd footnote to this adventure: six months

after we survived the Kern, the greatest river-rafting movie of all time, *Deliverance*, was released. I had a real visceral empathy with the film's characters and their experience. Thankfully, unlike those men, I never encountered any rapist hillbillies. The river was traumatizing enough.

CHAPTER 29

My First Mentor

 The guest star roles that I'd recently filmed aired on TV in quick succession, and my work garnered good reviews. Producers and casting directors took notice that I could play a range of characters with dramatic depth. I was being asked to audition for roles in major films like *American Graffiti* and *The Last Detail* with Jack Nicholson. I didn't get parts in either of those projects, but it was good to know that people saw that I could play someone other than nerdy Ernie Douglas.

I wanted to build on this new credibility, so I searched for an acting teacher who could help me grow as an artist. That person was a man named Jack Garfein. He was a prominent member of the New York Actors Studio and founded the school's Los Angeles branch before creating his own academy, the Actors and Directors Lab. The Lab became my second home.

Garfein's lessons taught his students to be observers of human behavior and practitioners of emotional honesty. His appreciation of great paintings, musical symphonies, and dance companies was infectious. The acting technique he taught was simple and practical based on the teachings of the American Stanislavski disciples: Lee Strasberg, Uta Hagen, Sandy Meisner, and Harold Clurman, Garfein's mentor.

During my time at the Lab, many world-class artists who were Garfein's personal friends taught there. Guest instructors included the famous mime Marcel Marceau, the brilliant teacher/actress Stella Adler, and the legendary Harold Clurman, cofounder of the seminal Group Theatre. Even the infamous cult novelist Henry Miller came to our school to talk about his life and work. These people were giants in their respective arts, and it was a privilege to hear them discuss their work in an intimate setting.

Sensing my seriousness, Jack offered me a couple of plum opportunities. One assignment was to stage-manage Henry Miller's lectures. This gave me a chance to talk with the literary giant, one on one. Granted, they were hardly profound meetings of the minds; it was nothing more than idle chitchat, mainly about his attraction to Japanese women and his love of Ping-Pong. Nonetheless, it was conversation with one of the most influential literary lions of the twentieth century. On the day of Miller's first lecture at the Lab, the author's presence nearly created a riot when dozens of his devoted fans grew angry because they were denied entry to the sold-out event and started pounding on the theater doors. Miller insisted that the rabble outside be let in. "To hell with the fire codes," the great man bellowed. Miller was a subversive, a man of the people, and the doors were flung open to one and all.

Garfein gave me another choice assignment: driving Harold Clurman around town. I would drive him up to Brando's compound on Mulholland Drive or to a dinner party at Stella Adler's house. Basically, I was a "fly on the wall" when accompanying Clurman on these outings, and rightly so. I was a young man and definitely out of my league among these legends. It was best to just sit and listen.

I spent the next year at the Actors and Directors Lab, working on scenes from modern classic plays to Shakespeare, sharpening my acting skills, and gaining confidence in my abilities. I was no James Dean or Marlon Brando, but I was learning to express my own voice in my work.

My next big acting break let me test my newly acquired skills. I was cast in a lead role in a new one-hour dramatic series, *Sons and Daughters*. I was ready to take the next step into my adult career and leave my child actor days behind.

CHAPTER 30

Starring in a New TV Series

Sons and Daughters focused on a group of high school friends growing up in the 1950s. *American Graffiti* had just struck box-office gold and tapped into the country's longing to relive all things Eisenhower. It was now the early 1970s, and the country was fatigued by the Vietnam War and stunned by the Watergate political scandals. Audiences were craving the soothing balm of nostalgia. Chuck Berry, hot rods, and malt shops were hip again.

I was cast as Moose Kerner, a 1950s nerd, and starred in the series with Gary Frank (later of *Family*), Scott Colomby (*Caddyshack*), and Glynnis O'Connor, a beautiful, sensitive young actress whom I had a tremendous crush on. Everybody did.

Sons and Daughters was a high-quality drama, full of teenage angst and despair. That was our big distinction from *American Graffiti*. Unfortunately, the drama aspect was also the show's downfall. Audiences wanted their 1950s entertainment served up with a cherry Coke and apple pie, not cancer and unwanted pregnancies. We had the right era, just the wrong tone. Another show set in the 1950s came on that same year, too, and it turned out to be exactly what people wanted: *Happy Days*. Right era, right tone, and, especially, the right ratings. That show was on TV for the next eleven years.

We did thirteen glorious episodes full of betrayal, turmoil, and melodrama before we were canceled. I certainly got an opportunity to exercise my newfound acting chops. I also got a chance to work with Richard Donner who directed the pilot and a few of the series' episodes. Donner later directed *Superman*, the first movie with Christopher Reeve, and rebooted the entire franchise. He also did all of the *Lethal Weapon* films and many other blockbusters.

Donner was a big man with a big personality and a huge booming baritone voice. If he didn't like your work in a scene he'd bellow, *"Energy, Energy! Cut ten minutes out of it!"* I learned that he wasn't being mean, just honest, a quality that I liked.

Over time, I learned that Donner loved practical jokes. This being the case, I got an artist friend to draw a huge poster of Donner having sexual intercourse with a woman. Stagehands hung it from the top rafters of our cavernous soundstage, and we brought him in for the presentation blindfolded. The second I uncovered his eyes, stagehands illuminated the billboard-size work of art. Donner exploded in laughter at the sight of the woman having sex with him, mainly because she was screaming the words: *"Energy, Energy! Cut ten minutes out of it!"*

I tried to pull another prank on Donner, but, unfortunately, it backfired. I snuck into his trailer with a willing female co-conspirator; we stripped off our clothes and climbed onto his sofa, me on top. Gary Frank had written in lipstick on one butt cheek: "Moose Loves Donner." When Dick entered his trailer and saw us, he roared with laughter. Then he grabbed me by the arm and dragged me outside the trailer. Now the joke was on me. I was standing stark naked on a busy lunch-hour street at Universal Studios, the lot with tour buses full of gawking fans.

I ran like Wile E. Coyote with his ass on fire, trying to make it to my dressing room, which was about a city block away. My situation got really dire when a tram loaded with tourists turned a corner and our paths were going to cross. I could see the headlines: CHILD ACTOR RUNS AMUCK IN THE NUDE! Or even worse: ERNIE EXPOSES HIMSELF!

Thinking fast, I leaped into somebody's unlocked Mercedes that was parked on the street. As the tram passed and the tourists gawked, I waved and scrunched my naked body down to keep from being seen. Once they were gone, I streaked (literally) to my room. That was the last time I tried to play a prank on Donner.

Once *Sons and Daughters* was officially canceled, I was at another crossroads. College seemed less of an option now that I was working regularly in television. I still wanted to improve as an actor, though, and the challenge of TV work seemed limited.

I remembered the advice that Roddy McDowall gave me while working on *The Elevator*. McDowall was a child actor from the golden era of movies and had transitioned into a very successful adult actor. His words echoed in my head: "Go to New York and work on the stage. That's what I did."

I'd been in love with New York and the theater forever, so McDowall's suggestion only whetted my appetite to move there. I figured that if I didn't do it now, I would probably never go. So I packed my bags and headed east.

CHAPTER 31

The Skin of Our Teeth

 My plan was to stay with my Uncle Bernard for a couple of months and look for a New York agent to represent me. Despite my recent TV successes, I wasn't sure if the East Coast theater crowd would embrace me. They are a pretty elitist group. I was afraid they'd think that I was just another TV child star whose best days were behind him. I just didn't know what to expect.

The first meeting I had was with Stark Hesseltine, a top theatrical agent. I told him I was ready to set down roots in the city and commit myself to the theater. Hesseltine couldn't have been more supportive or receptive. In fact, he had an audition for me to go on that very day. Whoa, that's fast, I thought to myself, feeling a bit nervous. I wanted to show him that I was game, though, and agreed to go.

The audition was for the part of the Messenger Boy in the Thornton Wilder play, *The Skin of Our Teeth*. The play was being produced by the Kennedy Center to celebrate the upcoming Bicentennial Birthday of America. It was being touted as the biggest, most prestigious production that year. The stars in it were Elizabeth Ashley, red hot having just done *Cat on a Hot Tin Roof* on Broadway; Alfred Drake, legendary Broadway musical star; and Martha Scott, who played Emily in the original production of Wilder's most famous play, *Our Town*. If that wasn't enough pressure, José Quintero was directing the play. He was a cofounder of the Circle in the Square Theatre in 1951, which many consider to be the birth of the Off Broadway theater scene. Quintero was also responsible for mounting the first important productions of Eugene O'Neil's plays in America. He was a true theater legend.

I ran to a bookstore, got a copy of *Skin,* read it, and dashed off to my meeting with Mr. Quintero. While the messenger boy wasn't a starring role, the character did have an important four-page scene where he was the focus of the action. I prepped for the reading and sat in the casting office, trying to keep relaxed and focused. I also had a book with me, Henry Miller's *Tropic of Cancer.* I hadn't read it yet, but I thought I'd keep it visible when I met with Quintero. One of my biggest fears was being perceived as a flakey TV actor from Hollyweird. I hoped that just the sight of the book in my hands might enhance my intellectual stature. I was looking for any edge I could find, no matter how superficial. At last, a casting assistant called my name.

I entered an inner office to find Quintero sitting alone. The usual anonymous faces, other producers and casting directors, were oddly absent from the audition room. Quintero rose to his feet and extended his hand to greet me. He was a big man of Panamanian descent with dark bronzed skin and a pearly white smile. He immediately noticed *Tropic of Cancer* in my hands, and his face lit up.

"How do you like the book?" he said.

Uh-oh. The book was just going to be a prop, something to burnish my intellectual image. Now the director wanted to discuss it in depth. *What the hell was I thinking? This was going to be my undoing.*

I responded with some generic praise and quickly shifted the conversation over to Henry Miller's lectures that I stage-managed at my old acting school. The conversation mercifully veered into questions about Jack Garfein, whom Quintero knew.

We had a lively talk about our mutual friend, and I started to relax, enjoying the chat.

I've always felt that a little animated conversation at an audition helps to book the job. It lets people in the room see who you really are. On the other hand, if the schmoozing goes on too long, you can lose your focus on the all-important reading. An actor never lands a role because his anecdotes were better than his reading. At last the conversation came to a lull, and I figured it was time we got to work.

Quintero studied me with his piercing brown eyes, like a poker player holding all the aces. The silence started to feel awkward. I lifted my play, ready to read my scene with him.

He finally said, "Very nice to meet you. Thank you for coming in."

My heart dropped like an anchor. *What? No reading? What's going on?*

Quintero thanked me a second time. When the director thanks you for coming, not just once but twice, he is saying you should leave the room, now.

I understood the *audition-speak* and stood up, shell-shocked. I shuffled out of the room without reading a single line of dialogue. I'd failed at my first and, probably last, New York audition.

I walked up Broadway in a daze, heading back to my uncle's place on West End Avenue and 71st Street. I replayed the meeting in my mind. *What did I do wrong? He must've seen some flaw in my character.* I was, after all, flaunting a book that I'd never read. That was dumb. My shame shifted to anger. At least they let you *read* your audition scene at Hollywood interviews. Even if you're a moron, they give you your shot. New York was even tougher and colder than I'd heard.

I entered my uncle's apartment and flopped onto the sofa, numb from Quintero's sucker-punch. The phone's answering machine had a red light blinking, so I pushed the playback button.

Stark Hesseltine's voice crackled, "Barry, they want to book you for the role you read for in *The Skin of Our Teeth.* Give me a call. Congratulations."

I said aloud, "The part I read for? I didn't read for anything!"

I was shell-shocked, again, in a good way this time. I couldn't believe it. I played the message two more times to confirm what I'd heard, and it started to sink in: *The first New York audition I ever went to, for the biggest production of the year, and I got it! Damn!*

Then, insecurity replaced my elation. I wondered if Quintero realized that I've never done any professional theater work before. I'd been in a couple of high school plays and did scenes galore at the Actors and Directors Lab, but that was nothing compared to being in the biggest play of the upcoming Broadway season. I got the shivers.

My Uncle Bernard came home and I announced the news. Being a lifelong New Yorker and very knowledgeable about the theater, he tried to put my fears to rest.

"Quintero never has an actor read for a role," he said. "It's belittling. If the casting director brings you in to meet him, he assumes you've got talent. You're going to do fine."

I tried to take his encouragement to heart, but the goose bumps remained.

I found out later that my uncle was right about Quintero. He doesn't have actors *read* for him. He's more interested in the person's character and personality, hoping it will fit the role he's trying to fill.

Apparently, Quintero saw something in me that fit Messenger Boy, a character who is a bit of a braggart and an exaggerator. Maybe he could tell that I hadn't read *Tropic of Cancer* after all. Whatever the case, I was headed for Broadway.

Rehearsals commenced four weeks later. The first morning we sat in a big circle. José announced that he had no great vision or personal theme that he wanted to impose on us. It wasn't a confession of inadequacy or lack of intellectual perception. His plan was to find the reality of the play as our rehearsals evolved, through our mutual exploration of Thornton Wilder's words. The end result would be organic and truthful. This was the process that Quintero used on all of his plays. It became clear that this was not going to be a network TV kind of experience.

The first reading of the play by the actors began, and I was all eyes and ears. Elizabeth Ashley approached her role with Southern sass and free-flowing intensity. She was playing the part of Sabrina, the outspoken maid who lives with the play's Antrobus family.

Alfred Drake was cast as Mr. Antrobus. Known best for his work in musicals like *Kismet* and *Oklahoma!* Drake read his words as if reading notes off a musical chart, going high and then low. Frankly, he gave his best performance on that first day. Not much changed after that.

Martha Scott, who was playing Mrs. Antrobus, projected an earth mother quality, grounded yet playful.

Steve Railsback was cast in the pivotal role of the son, Henry Antrobus, a part that was originally played by Montgomery Clift in the first *Skin* production in the 1940s. Railsback impressed me the most in that first reading. He had a brooding, dangerous aura that was perfect for the role Henry, a character that was a surrogate for the Bible's evil son, Cain. Railsback's charisma and explosive anger served him well years later when he stunned television audiences playing Charles Manson in the TV mini-series, *Helter Skelter.*

After the reading, I wanted to get to know Railsback better. He seemed to be the cast member closest to my age. I was hoping to make a friend, or it was going to be a long, lonely journey. After a bit of small talk, Railsback asked if I wanted to go with him to a surprise birthday party at the Actors Studio where he was a member. I was hesitant, not knowing the guest of honor. Railsback assured me it would be okay. I asked who the party was for.

"Elia Kazan," he said.

Elia Kazan? Director of *A Street Car Named Desire, On the Waterfront,* and *East of Eden*? One of the greatest film directors of all time? Hell, yes, I'd like to go to the party!

Going inside the New York Actors Studio on 44th Street was like entering the Vatican of acting schools. This was the training ground for so many great artists: James Dean, Marlon Brando, Marilyn Monroe, Al Pacino; the list of former well-known students goes on and on. The place reeks of history and importance.

We located Kazan. The party had already begun, and actors and actresses surrounded the director. Some of the guests were famous faces while others were up-and-comers like Harvey Keitel, Treat Williams, and Mickey Rourke. Kazan greeted Railsback like a son. The great director had, in fact, discovered Railsback and given him his first lead role in the film *The Visitors*. What an amazing day: Broadway rehearsals in the morning, parties for Kazan in the afternoon.

After the party, Railsback and I taxied across town to the East Side. His girlfriend, Wendy Sherman, cooked us dinner, a healthy organic cheese and onion pie. Over our meal, he confessed that he was a huge fan of *My Three Sons* when he was growing up in Texas. He said that he couldn't believe his eyes when he saw me sitting among the cast members earlier that day. That caught me by surprise. I have always been so naive about the impact of *Sons*. He sounded more in awe of me than I was of him. That day was the beginning of another hugely influential and important friendship. Railsback became a great inspiration, in my acting and in my life. He still is.

Rehearsals plowed forward. One of the biggest problems Quintero faced was blending the different acting styles among the show's stars. Elizabeth Ashley was mercurial, unpredictable, and prone to improvise upon Wilder's text. She was crafting a character that existed in her own universe. In contrast, Martha Scott was religiously faithful to Wilder's words and thrived on what the other actors were giving. Alfred Drake was working in his own vacuum, too. From day one, his performance seemed as choreographed and preplanned as a dance step. Once he had rehearsed a scene a couple of times, his performance hardened like cement. Railsback, on the other hand, was full of real emotion and spontaneity, having trained at the Actors Studio.

After work one day, Railsback told me that he accidentally stepped on Drake's foot in a scene they were rehearsing. The grand old man of musical theater didn't bat an eyelash, completely ignoring the fact that his shoe was pinned to the floor. Steve said he purposely pressed harder with his boot to see if he could get a reaction from Drake, anything that resembled human emotion. The elder actor ignored the pain and plowed ahead, singing his lines without a care in the world. Not exactly "in the moment" acting.

As for my big scene, I was the Messenger Boy who bursts into the Antrobuses' home to warn them about the dangers of a new ice age that's occurring. For those of you who've never read *The Skin of Our Teeth,* the play follows the Antrobus family through the trials of three historical epochs: act one takes place during the ice age; act two is in modern times at a Shriner's convention where corruption and vice run amuck; act three is set in the future, after the apocalypse.

Quintero wanted me to enter my scene with great urgency; the glacial ice was only blocks away from the Antrobus home and about to swallow it up.

The first time I performed my scene, I gave myself an imaginary prior circumstance (an actor's device). I envisioned a pack of feral dogs chasing me to the Antrobuses' front door, hoping this might energize me with a sense of panic. I made my entrance in the scene and barely got two words of dialogue out of my mouth before Quintero held up his hand.

"Hold on, Barry. I want you to make your entrance again, with more urgency this time."

I nodded and went offstage. This time I pictured a gang of thugs, cold and hungry, roughing me up. I imagined escaping from them and running to the Antrobus house to take refuge . . . and then I burst onto the stage to begin the scene. I got through my first speech about the massive glaciers, and then Quintero stopped me again.

"Stop, please. Barry, I need to really feel how dire your situation is. It's not quite there yet. Do it over."

I nodded obediently, but I could feel a knot in my stomach tightening. The director wanted something from me, and I was not delivering.

I did the entrance a couple more times, trying to add more prior circumstances. I combined the angry thugs with the feral dogs, and threw in a charging herd of wooly mammoths, too. Still, Quintero wasn't satisfied.

Quintero came up onto the set and wrapped an arm around my shoulder. I thought he was going to escort me to the nearest exit. Instead, he smiled, mischief in his eyes.

"I want you to try something, Barry," Quintero said, giggling. "Run."

"Uh . . . run? Right here?" I asked.

"Yes. Run. Go . . . Now!" Quintero replied.

I looked out at the entire company of actors who were sitting in the audience watching. I felt like running . . . right out the door. I started to jog around the stage.

"Faster!" Quintero barked.

I ran faster.

"Jump over those chairs!" Quintero said. "Don't stop tell I tell you."

I jumped and ran around the stage as Quintero went back into the audience to watch the action.

Quintero watched me leap chairs and tear around the stage for a few more minutes and then he yelled, "Okay, Barry, now make your entrance!"

I went right into the scene, huffing and puffing, trying to catch my breath as I spoke of the advancing ice and the people suffering. Instinctively, I flopped down exhausted on a sofa next to Sabrina (Ashley's character) and started to flirt with her! Our world was supposedly freezing over, but I still had time for carnal thoughts about the sexy maid. It was an odd moment, but human and amusing. All kinds of interesting behavior evolved out of that simple but brilliant direction.

When the scene finished and I made my exit, Quintero led the cast in applause. Lesson learned.

We had four more weeks of rehearsals in New York and two weeks of out-of-town performances in Birmingham, Alabama. Despite Quintero's directorial skill and Wilder's brilliant words, the play was a chaotic mess. The warring acting styles of the stars certainly contributed to the difficulties. More than that, *Skin* is a damn hard piece of theater to mount. Previous productions, with stellar casts that included Fredric March, Tallulah Bankhead, and Montgomery Clift, all failed to master the play's challenging structure, which unfolds like an evening of one-acts, each one being set in a different epoch. We were in a constant struggle to bring the creative elements together, performances and the written word. Occasionally the play gelled, but nobody seemed to know why or how to recreate the magic.

As for my work in the play, I was having a ball playing to live audiences for the first time. Quintero certainly had other bigger problems to focus on, but he took time to critique my work every night. He liked everything I was doing except for the last sentence in my final speech. In that particular passage, I recited the many different ways that information is disseminated: from word of mouth, to newspapers, radios, and TV, all of man's amazing inventions. I was excited as hell in my delivery, and Quintero approved. When it came to the final line, "What hath God wrought?" the director wasn't satisfied. He wanted to hear wonder and awe in my voice, and I wasn't getting it.

To help me discover what was missing, Quintero would cite personal experiences to illuminate the feeling. That was his favorite directorial method with actors. He told me how it felt coming to New York City from rural Panama and seeing the blazing, electric power of Times Square: "What hath God wrought?" Another night he spoke to me about a newsreel that showed a fiery atom bomb exploding and its subsequent devastation: "What hath God wrought?" All his examples were evocative, and each night I'd try to make them my own.

After the show, Quintero would grin and say, "You were quite good tonight, except for the last line about . . . " That was the routine that followed practically every preview performance. I wanted to please him, but no matter what I tried, the line reading was not quite right. It was driving me nuts.

After two weeks of shows in Birmingham, we boarded a plane to take us to Washington, D.C., and I was still grappling with the dreaded line. As I looked out the window of the flying aircraft, gazing at the patchwork of farmland and twisting rivers far below, I felt a tap on my shoulder. It was Quintero.

"We're flying at thirty thousand feet at five hundred miles per hour. Birds can't even keep up!" the director said, shaking his head. "Imagine that? . . . What hath God wrought?" His eyes twinkled, passing along yet another note about my troubled line.

It was an "ah-ha!" kind of moment for me. Something clicked, and from then on I nailed the line in most every performance. Quintero would grin and nod afterward. What a gentle and persistent soul he was.

We began our final week of previews in Washington, D.C., before the gala opening at the Kennedy Center. The play was still a hodge-podge theatrical event, wildly out of sync in the acting department.

Not only was the play on unsteady ground, our inspired leader, Quintero, was about to fall off the wagon. He had a notorious history of alcoholism and started work on *Skin* sober and clear headed. As stress of the production mounted, you could see his hands quivering from the nervous tremors.

It's probably not fair to point fingers at anyone and say they were the cause of his fall. Nonetheless, Liz Ashley's liberties with the play's text were driving poor Quintero crazy. Every night in previews, she'd eat up more and more scenery, strutting around in a skimpy maid's outfit that was straight out of a cheap porno flick. Her hammy performance, complete with ad libs and winks to the audience, was shifting the focus of the play onto her character rather than the plight of the Antrobus family. Quintero tried hard to rein her in, hoping to get some balance in the show, but Ashley was beyond direction. She was doing a solo act, and the other actors were just props in her burlesque performance.

Opening night finally arrived, and we had one of our better nights. The show actually came together in some weird way. Call it luck, opening-night energy, whatever, but the play had drive and purpose, and the audience loved it.

The major newspapers gave *Skin* decent reviews and heaped praise upon Ashley for her over-the-top performance. Perhaps she realized that the only way for our disjointed production to succeed was to go bonkers onstage every night.

Of course, that's not the way Quintero saw it. He truly felt that her performance was distorting the play. The more Quintero begged her to tone it down, the more Ashley ad-libbed, particularly now that the critics had validated her instincts.

Quintero couldn't take it anymore. He sold his interest in the show and formally announced he would be leaving. His work as director was done, and now the play belonged to the players. It was like having your father tell you he's moving away and that your crazy Aunt Liz will be in charge now. We gulped and prepared for a wild ride.

From then on, every actor was looking out for himself. If you saw the play on Friday and again on Saturday, you'd see a different performance. Luckily, our run in Washington didn't depend on media reviews or sold-out shows to survive. There was big money behind the play. It was the Kennedy Center's celebration of our country's two hundredth birthday. Nobody wanted to see the first gala show disappear in a week or two. That would have looked utterly unpatriotic.

We marched forward for another six weeks of performances. No matter what dramas were occurring onstage or backstage, I was having a blast.

Working at the Kennedy Center had other perks, too. One of my favorite things to do was watch the great ballet dancers Margo Fonteyn and Rudolf Nureyev perform at the opera house. After performing my big scene in act one, I had about forty-five minutes to kill until I came on again in the second act as a drunken conventioneer (I did two other smaller roles in addition to the Messenger Boy).

I'd sneak over to the opera house through an underground tunnel and stand in the wings to observe the artists at work. It's one thing to watch a performer from the audience and a totally different experience to see them backstage. You're privy to all kinds of behind-the-scenes technical glitches or moments of personal trouble. Occasionally, you see a performer looking fabulous onstage and moments later rush into the wings and barf up their lunch.

Nureyev was a defector from the communist Soviet Union and is considered by many to be the greatest ballet dancer of the twentieth century. He also had a reputation for slapping stagehands whenever he felt he was giving a dull, pedestrian performance. These unprovoked assaults gave him an adrenaline rush that would pump up his pirouettes. Nice for Nureyev, not so good for the stagehand. I kept this fact in mind every time the mercurial Russian was backstage. He frequently gave me the stink eye, and my presence must have been quite the mystery to him.

I'd appear backstage at the opera house at the same time every day, watch the great dancer at work for fifteen minutes, and then disappear back to my theater. Perhaps Nureyev thought I was a KGB agent plotting to whisk him back to mother Russia. He rarely took his eye off me, and I never took my eye off him.

After Nureyev's show closed, I told Railsback about my tense silent relationship with the dancer. He figured that Nureyev probably recognized me from *My Three Sons*. That theory seemed pretty far fetched. Years later, though, I read an interview with Nureyev. He said that he learned to speak English by watching American TV shows, one of his favorites being *MTS*. Weird.

The Skin of Our Teeth was nearing the end of its run at the Kennedy Center, and the show's future was in doubt. We were hoping to go straight to Broadway. Unfortunately, our mixed D.C. reviews didn't warrant it. The producers made a bold decision: we would go to Boston and hope to get more reviews that would be good enough to carry us into New York. Fine by me, I wasn't ready to throw in the towel, either.

I decided I needed a break from the company, so I booked a sleeper berth on a train rather than travel with the rest of the actors by plane. This led to one of the wildest, most erotic nights of my life.

I'd always loved trains, having crossed the country twice in the 1960s with my mom and brother on the Santa Fe Super Chief. I arrived early in the evening at the D.C. train station ready to roll. Unfortunately, the train wasn't; its air-conditioning system was broken and workers were trying to fix it.

The August temperature was over 100 degrees, hot and humid. As a courtesy to the stranded passengers, the railroad was offering free sodas at the bar, which is where I met two girls, Carey and Sara. They were Midwest farm girls about my age, unpretentious and attractive in their faded blue jeans and Ohio State T-shirts. They told me that they'd been hitchhiking across the country until their paths crossed with a man named Peter, who happened to be the president of the railroad. The girls were traveling on board the train as his guests.

The railroad president; this could be interesting, I thought. I mopped my sweaty brow and asked, "Where is Peter now?"

"Oh, he's under the train fixing the air-conditioner," Carey said. She twirled the end of her straight brown hair playfully and smiled.

"He's fixing it . . . himself?" I said. I got the vibe that Peter must be a real character.

"He's crazy about trains," Sara added.

At the other end of the crowded club car, I heard a man's voice with a nasal Bostonian accent call out, "The compressor's broke and I couldn't fix it. Darn it!" A tall man in his forties, wearing a dark pinstripe suit, was carving his way through a herd of thirsty passengers.

"Peter! Over here!" Carey called out.

As he got closer, I got a better look at the railroad president. I had imagined I'd meet a trim, silver-haired, square-jawed man of distinction. Not so with Peter. He was big and dumpy like Baby Huey, round and wide at the waist, narrow at the shoulders. His jowly cheeks swallowed up his oversized pouting lips. Peter slapped impatiently at the dirt still clinging to the knees of his suit pants.

"Are you okay, Peter?" Carey asked gingerly.

"Damned compressor broke again!" he snapped. "I just had it replaced, too!" His cheeks flushed red with embarrassment, like a spoiled child whose favorite toy was broken. "I'm very, very sorry."

The girls exchanged timid looks, not sure how to calm their pouting host. He grumped, "We'll be leaving the station momentarily, without cool air!"

Right on cue, the train lurched forward. Peter glanced at me, suddenly aware that I was with his female companions. His hangdog expression brightened. *"My Three Sons,* right?" he blurted out.

I nodded, relieved to see his sour puss lighten. It's always surprising how fast a person's mood can change after meeting someone famous. It's like a magic tonic. He looked around the packed club car and said, "Let's go to my compartment. Would you like to have a drink with us there?"

I smiled and thought, Would I like to have drinks with the

railroad president and two really cute girls from Ohio? . . . oh, sure, why not?

We arrived at Peter's compartment; it was actually two sleeper suites combined to make one spacious stateroom. Cold beer was delivered and I guzzled mine like water. It was hot as hell, even in the president's suite. When Peter found out that I played guitar, he insisted that I bring it back to his room so we could have a sing-a-long. When the president makes a request, you oblige.

I retrieved my Gibson from my berth and returned to play every Beatles, Rolling Stones, and Simon & Garfunkel tune that I knew. The more cold beer we drank, the louder our sing-a-long became.

At about eleven o'clock, there was a knock on the compartment door. The president, now pretty sloshed, cracked open the door to find an old black porter smiling sheepishly. He whispered, "It's past eleven o'clock, sir, and some passengers are startin' to complain 'bout the music."

Peter nodded, then slurred, "We'll take our singing somewhere else then." He looked at us, lifted a plump index finger, and pointed it at the door a few times. We took this as a signal that we were leaving.

Moments later, our drunken host led us down a corridor toward the front of the train. I was right behind him, clutching my Gibson, trying not to bounce off the walls as the train swayed back and forth. The girls brought up the rear, carrying cases of beer.

Our trek ended on a clanging, wind-blown platform between cars. A steel door with a sign that said U.S. MAIL CAR—AUTHORIZED PERSONNEL ONLY prevented us from going any farther. Peter rapped repeatedly on the metal door, muttering curses about how it was hurting his knuckles. Eventually a peephole in the door slid open, and a pair of squinty eyes studied us.

"I need to come in," Peter announced with authority.

The man behind the door said, "You can't come in unless you're mail personnel. It's against the law."

Irritated, Peter slammed an I.D. badge up against the peephole and bellowed, "This is my train, open the goddamn door!"

The peephole shut. Carey and I exchanged puzzled looks as we swayed with the jiggling platform. The door remained closed, and I assumed a debate was occurring inside the mail car. Suddenly the portal swung open, and a mail worker waved us in. Peter, smug and satisfied, marched forward and we followed.

The mail car was crammed with stacked cardboard boxes and gray duffel bags marked u.s. MAIL. Probably because of the stifling heat, the loading door was slid open to let some air in, and the outside scenery rushed by in a blur.

Three nondescript mail clerks gawked at us. We must have looked like an odd apparition appearing out of nowhere. They looked nervous, and I'm sure they felt their jobs were at risk.

"Go back to work. We'll be gone soon. Nobody will know," Peter said, waving them away. "Sit, play, sing!" he instructed us.

I parked my butt on some duffel bags, positioned my guitar, and resumed the concert with the Beatles song "You've Got to Hide Your Love Away." We joined off-key voices again as the train's constant clatter provided us rhythm. What an amazing, surreal scene.

Our revelry continued for a couple more hours until my throat was raw and raspy from singing. My brain was swimming in beer, too, as I grandly bid adieu to the president, his female companions, and, of course, the slack-jawed mail clerks. I stumbled toward the door, and Carey jumped to her feet. She said she was exhausted, too, and wanted to go to sleep. The night, already memorable, was about to take a turn for the erotic.

Carey and I had been eyeing each other all evening. The moment we were away from the others, we locked lips in a heated embrace. I suddenly wasn't as exhausted as I thought; youthful hormones are such wonderful things.

Carey and I rushed to my sleeping berth, which was an upper bunk separated from the corridor by a heavy curtain. We tore off each other's clothes and made passionate, over-heated love all through New York and Connecticut. Our lust was finally exhausted in Massachusetts as the sun rose and we fell asleep.

As the train neared the Boston train station, Carey and I awoke to the porter's voice announcing the train's arrival. We dragged ourselves out of bed, hungover as hell, and stumbled to the president's stateroom.

We knocked on his door, and Peter opened it, greeting us with a stony glare. "Morning," he hissed, making no attempt to hide his displeasure. His puffy bloodshot eyes narrowed with disdain, and he wobbled woozily back to a sofa. Sara was shrunk down in a seat across from Peter, unwilling to make eye contact with us.

It was hard to read what was behind this cold reception. Perhaps the president was worried about Carey's disappearance. She offered up an apology, but he rejected it with a grunt and stared sullenly out the stateroom's window.

My beer-pickled brain went from throbbing to pounding. I started to sweat, and it wasn't from the lack of air-conditioning. I wondered, Maybe he's jealous that I'd slept with one of his concubines.

That didn't make sense, though. Carey told me that Peter gave no indication of wanting sex from her or Sara in the two weeks they'd been together. She assumed he was just a lonely, rich eccentric who wanted company.

I wanted to leave the room, but there was no easy way to make a graceful exit. Mercifully, the train clanged to a stop in Boston.

Our group, festive and merry the night before, disembarked from the train in complete silence. We walked together through the bustling station like total strangers.

At the curb outside, I hopped into the first available taxi. Peter gave me a stiff handshake and then quickly looked away.

My eyes connected with Carey's. I could see that she hoped we could meet up again, but she couldn't say so in front of Peter. She wasn't done riding the president's *gravy train.*

As my cab inched away from the curb, I glanced back at the trio, and something really odd occurred: Peter looked at me and raised the middle digit of his left hand. I couldn't believe my eyes; the railroad president was giving me the finger. It was such an unexpected farewell gesture that I had to laugh. What a weird ending to a wonderful night.

I'd never been to Boston before, so I was eager to experience this historic city. Not knowing much about the lay of the land, Railsback and I chose to stay at the Avery Hotel just off the Commons, the city's grand park. It was also within walking distance of our new theater, the Colonial.

Soon after moving in, I learned that my new neighborhood was called the Combat Zone, an area rife with prostitution, drugs, and other assorted illegal mayhem. It felt like I'd moved to Tattoine and was staying at the Star War's Cantina. As Obi-Wan Kenobi said: "You will never find a more wretched hive of scum and villainy." That was a perfect description of my new home.

The Avery was a grand old hotel that had fallen on hard times. Every time you set foot outside, you had to dodge hookers in spandex hot pants, Super Fly drug dealers, and tattered beggars, every day and all night. It seemed strange that the city fathers of Boston, one of America's most Catholic and moral enclaves, would tolerate such a place.

Boston was a very conflicted town, and I soon learned that the Combat Zone was more than Babylon on steroids. It was also ground zero for a bitter civil rights battle between the city's African Americans and the white Irish communities. Large demonstrations filed past the Avery every few weeks, clamoring for freedom and equality. On one occasion, the march turned violent as the police started cracking heads with clubs. I watched the chaos from my fifth-story room window, witnessing a bloody uprising on the streets below, helpless to stop it.

It didn't take long to get infected with the callous and crazy vibe of the Zone, either. Some nights at three in the morning, I'd lean out my window and throw a half-eaten apple at the roof of a pimped-out Caddie on the street below. Other times, I'd drop a firecracker or two if the pimpmobile were blasting an annoying disco song. It's not normally my nature to do such things. I just got caught up in the madness. I was barely sane and mature, and caught up in a hostile, corrupt environment. It rubbed off.

Skin premiered in Boston, and the major papers saw a fairly coherent performance. Once again, the critics were mildly impressed with the play but loved Liz Ashley's Sabina. Maybe she did know better than any of us after all. Whatever the case, her bravura performance drew audiences, and that was enough to convince our financial backers to bring the play to New York. We would be going to Broadway after all.

Over the next six weeks in Boston, the show still didn't improve greatly. Without a director's input to guide us, we were floundering. Some nights were pretty good, some were pretty bad, others just pretty weird. Near the end of our run, though, we did have one truly exceptional performance, the night that Thornton Wilder, the play's renowned author, came to see the show.

Honestly, I didn't even know Mr. Wilder was still alive. Throughout his esteemed career, the Pulitzer Prize–winning writer never attended any productions of his works. For some reason, he had decided to break his lifelong rule and see our show. His attendance was going to be very special indeed. It was so noteworthy, in fact, that José Quintero rejoined our company to give notes. He implored Liz Ashley to do the play as Mr. Wilder had written it, no ad libs allowed!

The big night arrived, and Ashley was on her best behavior, performing the play verbatim. After the performance, Mr. Wilder, who was in his eighties, came up onstage and greeted each cast member with a smile and cooed, "Thank you, I enjoyed your performance tonight."

One funny, and perhaps telling, footnote regarding the sincerity of Mr. Wilder's praise involved my old buddy, Chris Craven. He was working up in Montreal, so I told him to come to Boston on the night that Mr. Wilder was attending. I figured he'd like to meet the author of *Our Town* since both of his uncles had starred in the original production decades ago.

To my surprise, Chris flew in on the big night and finagled his way backstage during intermission. After the show, we stood in the line of cast members to meet Mr. Wilder. Chris stepped up and extended his hand.

"Mr. Wilder, my name is Chris Craven. My Uncle Frank played the lead role of the stage manager in the very first production of *Our Town*, and my Uncle John was George Gibbs," Chris said.

The old man's tired eyes widened as if somebody poked him in the ribs. Wilder replied, "Oh, my goodness. That was in 1938! How are Frank and John?"

"Frank passed away, but Uncle John is alive and well in Barcelona," Chris said.

"Well, please send him my best regards," Wilder said. "And thank you for your performance tonight, Chris. I enjoyed you very much!"

Skin closed in Boston, and the producers announced that they had booked the only theater still available on Broadway, the Mark Hellinger. The more experienced members of the company groaned. The Hellinger was a huge, huge auditorium that held fifteen hundred seats and was best suited for large-scale musicals like *My Fair Lady* and *Jesus Christ Superstar.* A straight drama like *Skin* needed a more intimate space if we were to have any chance of pleasing the critics. All we could do now was cross our fingers.

Railsback and I rented a car and drove to New York. On the way, we stopped to visit Elia Kazan at his rustic farm in Connecticut. I was looking forward to spending time with him in a less chaotic setting than our previous meeting, his birthday party at the Actors Studio. Unfortunately, the director wasn't home when we arrived. His son, Chris Kazan, was, though.

Chris Kazan had written the film *The Visitors*, which Elia directed and Steve starred in. It's an overlooked Kazan classic about two Vietnam vets who've just been released from the brig. The soldiers pay a menacing visit to a former army buddy who testified against them in a My Lai–type massacre. The story is a brilliant and subtle study about young men struggling with the consequences of their violent actions.

Because the movie was shot on the director's property, I recognized many of the fictionalized settings. To my surprise, Kazan's house looked even more run-down than in the movie. The furniture was old and worn, screen doors were in need of repair, and the exterior paint was peeling. There was nothing that hinted of Kazan's Oscar-winning, international fame. The place was more hillbilly funk than Hollywood glitz.

Granted, my peek into the director's country retreat was about as superficial as it gets. I couldn't help wonder, though, if the home's shabby condition reflected the owner's depressed state of mind. Kazan had become a professional pariah, and his services were barely in demand anymore because of his involvement with Senator Joseph McCarthy and the blacklistings in the 1950s. Maybe cleaning house and putting on airs were never his style. Chalk up my observations to an overactive imagination.

We left Kazan's farm and drove south to the Big Apple. I felt a few butterflies when imagining the Broadway curtain going up. I thought I was prepared for the moment, though. After months of performances, I'd come a long way as a stage actor. I was ready to "hit the boards" in the big city.

The second I caught sight of Manhattan's skyscrapers, though, I felt terribly ill. Maybe I was in denial, repressing my fear, or maybe it was just a coincidence that I got nauseous. One way or the other, my brow heated up like a hot plate, and I felt like throwing up. I prayed that it was the lunch that we ate at Kazan's and not a real sickness.

By the time we arrived at my Uncle Bernard's apartment on the Upper Westside I was burning up and puking. It was the goddamn flu bug, for sure. I had five days to recover before we reopened on Broadway. That was going to be cutting it close, no matter how much Sprite, chicken soup, and vitamins I ingested.

I tried to nurse myself back into good health, but sure enough, I was running a temperature over a hundred degrees on opening night. My throat was so sore that I could barely speak. *The show must go on,* I reminded myself. That stupid saying had to have been invented by a producer. Nobody should ever have to perform when they're about to hurl big chunks and their head is filled with lava.

Somebody else by the name of Barry Livingston performed on opening night. It certainly didn't feel like me. I ran around the stage, in front of fifteen hundred people, in a fuzzy, dream-like state. The best that can be said is that I got through it. I was on autopilot and, amazingly, didn't crash. Friends and family told me afterward that I was good, but I didn't trust them. Most people, after witnessing a bad performance, will lie like some politicians to avoid speaking the painful truth. In my mind, Big Bird could have acted my part with more nuance and subtlety.

Fortunately, the show didn't live or die on my shoulders. Liz Ashley carried that load. As expected, she vamped and ad libbed wisecracks like crazy, hoping to pull off a miracle. The magic didn't happen, though. The theater gods, and the cavernous Mark Hellinger Theatre, swallowed us whole. The New York reviews were unanimously bad, and our days were numbered unless we could put fifteen hundred butts in our seats for every performance. That's hard enough to do with raves.

I recovered from the flu, and the show plowed ahead. We were hoping that good word-of-mouth might bring in the people and rescue us. Six weeks passed, but the people never came. *The*

Skin of Our Teeth was no more. It was an amazing, six-month journey that cemented my love of performing. I will carry that memory forever. It's high on my bucket list to get another chance to play on the Great White Way. Next time I hope I won't have dengue fever on opening night.

CHAPTER 32

Back to Los Angeles, Yawn

Once the play officially closed, I flew back to Los Angeles, eager to reunite with family and friends. I returned to a painful realization: everybody was stuck in the same place. My parents were still in the painful throes of their perpetual separation, and my friends were in a post–high school rut, smoking tons of weed and living on In-N-Out burgers. After my exhilarating East Coast experiences, the fun of "hanging out" with my Beret Brothers faded quickly. Nothing compared to the excitement of New York. There was a big dull void at the center of my life. I started to fill that hole with a new drug: cocaine.

If there ever was a *Lost Weekend* period of my life, this was it. Coke was the quick fix for every boring San Fernando Valley evening. The drug, once the exclusive high of rock stars and hipsters, was now available to everyone. Average Joe Suburb had joined the party.

You'd be offered a toot from your barber or from your auto mechanic, even at your lawyer's office. The white powder *snowed* at most every party, too. Bathroom doors would fly open, and sniffling people would exit with white rocks falling out of their noses. It became a badge of cool to whip out your vial, unscrew the black cap with the tiny brass spoon attached by a chain, and offer a hit of your "blow." You were just like Mick

Jagger—except he was doing pharmaceutical-grade coke, and the crap I bought was usually "stepped on" with laxatives. You'd snort a line, feel the first rush of the coke, and then fart like a Gerber baby.

I spent the next few years in self-destructive party mode. To give some balance to this chapter of my life, I should say that I held on to most of my money; I never shot anybody or robbed any convenience stores. I was twenty-two years old and uncertain about a lot of things: mainly who I was as a person and where I was headed as an artist. Coke was an artificial burst of excitement to fill a scary void.

Not long after my return to Los Angeles, I got a call from Steve Railsback who had remained in New York. He had been offered the role of Charles Manson in the miniseries *Helter Skelter* and wanted to know if he should accept the part. Railsback had real concerns regarding his safety. Charles Manson was in custody, but many of his murderous minions were still loose and making death threats to anybody participating in the upcoming movie. I grew up in Los Angeles and remember the horror of those grisly murders. It completely changed the way that hippies and counterculture types were perceived. The paranoia was real, and, of course, the media trumpeted every story about the Manson Family they could dig up.

Based on what I knew, I advised Railsback to *not* accept the role of Manson. The movie was probably going to be a huge hit, but it wasn't worth getting killed over. Railsback agreed and turned the Manson role down.

The director of *Helter Skelter,* Tom Gries, continued to pursue Railsback, though. He felt that Railsback was the only actor with the power and charisma to credibly play Manson. My pal also bore an eerie resemblance to the cult leader. Gries contacted Elia Kazan, Railsback's mentor, and pleaded with him to intervene. Kazan called Railsback up and told him to never be intimidated by anybody. "Fuck 'em all!" said Kazan. "Play Manson!"

Railsback accepted the role, giving perhaps the most convincing and human portrait of a madman ever put on film. Manson was a monster, but Railsback made his twisted, evil logic comprehensible. No small feat. Watching the movie today, it feels dated. Railsback's performance, though, is timeless and chilling.

Railsback came to L.A. to shoot *Helter Skelter,* and I hung out with him constantly at his new home, the Montecito Hotel in Hollywood. The hotel was every New York actor's favorite haunt when working in Hollywood.

I watched Railsback prepare to play Manson, and that included learning the cult leader's original songs. The studio got hold of one of Manson's demo cassettes and passed them on. The tapes were mostly hypnotic, droning blues rants. In all honesty, they weren't half bad, kind of like the early Rolling Stones. The chilling part was listening to the lead singer's snarling vocals and knowing this was the voice of pure evil.

Manson wanted to be a rock star and gave his music to Rudy Altobelli. He was a personal manager for talent in Hollywood and owned the house where the murders took place. When Altobelli rejected the songs, the cult leader ordered his followers to kill the manager at his home. Unbeknownst to Manson, though, Altobelli had moved out after leasing his residence to Sharon Tate. She had no connection to Manson whatsoever. The same was true for all the other innocent victims who were murdered at the house.

There was one other interesting aspect in this story. Soon after the murders in 1969, Altobelli moved back into his home and became Railsback's personal manager, frequently letting him stay at his house. When Railsback played Manson in the movie six years later, my actor pal had actually lived at the murder scene, not to mention having a relationship with the cult leader's prime target. Only in Hollywood.

CHAPTER 33

The Slow Slide into Oblivion

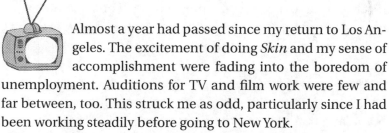 Almost a year had passed since my return to Los Angeles. The excitement of doing *Skin* and my sense of accomplishment were fading into the boredom of unemployment. Auditions for TV and film work were few and far between, too. This struck me as odd, particularly since I had been working steadily before going to New York.

My TV and film career prior to *Skin* seemed to be steaming along quite nicely and then, like the *Titanic*, I hit an uncharted iceberg in the black of night. I was entering a period where acting jobs just seemed to vanish. Of course, I didn't realize that my career was sinking until it was fully submerged.

It's hard to know what caused my stock to drop so abruptly. The easy answer would be to say that recreational drug use adversely affected my work. I honestly don't think drugs were a big factor. Perhaps it is denial to say that, but let me make a couple of points in my defense. Number one: I never snorted or inhaled anything illegal while I was working. Never. It wasn't because I was afraid of getting caught. I was paranoid about becoming dependent on a chemical to hot-wire my talent. That idea truly scared me, particularly if I couldn't get the specific drug I needed when the director yelled *Action!* Call it ego, but I wanted to believe it was me who was giving a good performance and not the pharmaceuticals. Number two: I never had any public relations disaster: drug busts, car crashes, or dalliances with cops pretending to be hookers. Those kinds of publicized mishaps can surely throw a career into a tailspin.

I was partying under the radar, doing about three grams of coke a week and steering clear of run-ins with the law. There were other factors, beyond my control, that I feel contributed to my career suddenly fading out.

About once every decade the television business (not so much film) evolves. A new edgy show arrives to change the landscape: *All in the Family* in the 1970s, *Dallas* in the 1980s, *Cosby* in the 1990s, Reality TV in the new millennium. If your big hit show is associated with a previous era, you can quickly become persona non grata when the next programming wave hits. Nobody wants to see an Edsel in a show full of shiny new Ferraris.

There is a way around this problem, though. It starts with talent and ends with the luck of being cast in something new and hot. When that happens, your membership in the "Hollywood hip club" is gladly renewed. It doesn't occur often, particularly with child stars who were series regulars. Ron Howard got that break going from *The Andy Griffith Show* to *Happy Days,* and look where it got him. Michael J. Fox went from TV's *Family Ties* to a feature film career. Neil Patrick Harris segued from *Doogie Howser, M.D.* to *How I Met Your Mother.*

I had a great opportunity at making the career leap forward with *Sons and Daughters.* Unfortunately, the series didn't fly and I was left in limbo . . . for a long, long while.

Unemployment can be a "good news/bad news" situation. The bad: it's a karate chop to one's self-esteem that can send you reeling into self-destruction. The good: it gives you plenty of time to find out what you are made of and build some character. My future was filled with both.

CHAPTER 34

Love at Long Last

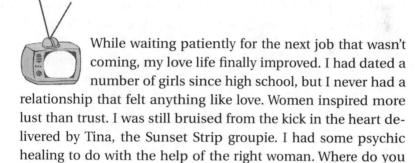 While waiting patiently for the next job that wasn't coming, my love life finally improved. I had dated a number of girls since high school, but I never had a relationship that felt anything like love. Women inspired more lust than trust. I was still bruised from the kick in the heart delivered by Tina, the Sunset Strip groupie. I had some psychic healing to do with the help of the right woman. Where do you find such a girl in the Hollywood jungle? Anywhere, everywhere, nowhere. Might as well start in a bar and hope to get lucky.

I was out drinking with my high school buddy Jeff Eget on a Saturday night. We wound up at Cyranos on the Sunset Strip, and I saw a girl walk in I recognized. It was Dale, the Ingrid Bergman look-alike from Ned Mandarino's acting class. I was too shy to let her know about my infatuation back then, but I wasn't going to make that mistake tonight.

We reunited over drinks and laughs. I got the feeling she was pretty happy to see me, too. Things were going great until a big glitch arose: her fiancé, Richard, joined us. She neglected to tell me about him.

Richard latched on to Dale's hand, said they had dinner reservations at a nearby bistro, and quickly led her out the door. In an instant, Dale reentered my life and was gone just as abruptly.

My heart sank as I looked out the bar's window and saw

Richard escorting Dale into a cozy little French restaurant across the street. Then, something possessed me: a swirling brew of ardor, booze, and insanity. This infernal love potion forced me to my feet, and I dashed out of the bar. *Damn the torpedoes!*

I weaved through the speeding cross-traffic on the Sunset Strip, ignoring the cacophony of honking horns, cursing drivers, and screeching tires. I was on a mission: to be with Dale or die. The latter option was closer than I'd realized.

Inside the bistro, I searched every nook and cranny until I found the couple at a cozy little table. Richard's jaw dropped. Dale smiled broadly, and that was as good an invitation as any for me to sit down.

To his credit, Richard kept his cool and at first seemed entertained by my drunken, foolish audacity. By the time the soup de jour arrived, Richard's amusement began to fade; he realized the fool wasn't leaving anytime soon. Not only that, I was eating his leftover appetizers.

Richard's face was growing redder, angrier. He tried to get me to leave with sarcastic put-downs about my rude manners and my child-acting career. The insults bounced off my ears like Ping-Pong balls. All I had to do was glance at Dale's amazed grin and I could withstand any verbal dagger Richard threw at me.

The party took a grimmer turn when my drunken pal, Jeff, tracked us down and sat at our table. One lovesick fool was barely tolerable; now his sidekick was here.

Trying to lighten things up, I proposed a toast to their pending marriage. Unfortunately, I clinked my wineglass against Richard's glass with too much gusto and it broke, splashing him with wine. The table went silent, and Dale's fiancé did a slow burn that would have made Jackie Gleason proud. My eyes were fixed on him, waiting for his next move.

Richard rose to his feet slowly, as if he were being inflated on the inside with hot air. He hovered over me, glowering, almost snarling. He fought the urge to tear my head off, angrily grabbed Dale's hand, and marched away from the table with her.

Of course, I had the unbelievably stupid instinct to give chase, again, but Jeff wisely held me in my seat. My pal convinced me that Dale's fiancé would surely knock out my front teeth if I pursued her.

Right on cue, Richard and Dale's fish dinners arrived. The waiter's grand presentation of the meals, to the wrong dinner guests, triggered gales of laughter. There was nothing to do now but chow down. In the end, I got stuck with a pretty hefty bill, which was cause for another crazy laugh. Served me right.

A few weeks later, my phone rang. It was Dale. The engagement was off and she was free to date. No risk, no gain.

Dale and I started dating, and the relationship quickly became romantic. She was the first woman who became my friend as much as a lover. This was a big emotional step for me. I finally started feeling like a man, not a boy anymore.

My new mature relationship triggered thoughts about marriage, kids, and a future without show business. If I didn't have an acting career, how would I make a living? Thank God for the *Sons* residuals that were paying my bills. Sooner or later, though, they were going to run out and I'd have to make a hard choice: abandon my acting aspirations and get a real job or starve.

For the moment, I was still in blissful denial, enthralled in a wonderful, new kind of romance.

CHAPTER 35

Big Changes for One and All

While I was basking in new love, my parents' stormy relationship finally came unglued: they separated. It was twenty years in the making, but it happened. My mom stayed at the family home in Studio City, and Dad was exiled to the Oak Wood Apartments, a sterile cluster of buildings overlooking Warner Bros. in Burbank. This sprawling hillside complex was a station for young actors looking for their big break, sex-hungry singles, and the severely depressed: the divorced and separated. Everyone wanted to be somewhere else, including my dad. He longed to be back home. That wasn't going to happen, because my mom was going solo, heading for a new planet.

Mother had hit fifty years of age and was in the throes of a full-fledged midlife crisis. She got a face-lift, bought hip-hugging spandex clothing, and made a new friend, a professional psychic named Dorothy Schwartz.

Schwartz was a chain-smoking Jewish yenta in her mid-sixties, about as tall as a hobbit and quite popular on the celebrity circuit for her predictions and advice. Her cigarette smoke–damaged voice rattled with phlegm, much like Andy Devine, the old Western movie star. She'd pop in for a daily visit with my mom flanked by Benny, her dim-witted forty-year-old son and Ida, her balding, orange-haired sister, another homunculus psychic. Bringing up the rear to this odd entourage was her driver, Doctor Gomez. His curly Mexifro hairdo and bushy mustache made him look like the Frito Bandito (or perhaps Gene Shalit, the *Today* show critic). He was once a successful plastic surgeon in Tijuana but currently was barred from practicing medicine for some unmentionable mishap. The cast of a Fellini film suddenly populated my old home.

Schwartz's psychic specialty was interpreting tarot cards. "Angel!" Schwartz would rumble with a frown while studying the cards. Angel was the new nickname Schwartz gave my mom. Her old nickname, Maryland, no longer fit. "Don't go back to Hilliard, Angel! He doesn't appreciate you. He doesn't see that you're an angel!"

I'd sit there, biting my tongue. My mom was pretty cool, but an angel? Okay. Whatever.

My mother absorbed Schwartz's every word as gospel. She seemed to be under her spell. Soon strange things started happening to the paintings that hung on the walls of the Milbank house. The names of the original artists had been painted over and the name Angel replaced them. It was clearly my mom's handiwork. I couldn't believe what she was doing. It wasn't that I cared about defaming our cheap works of art. Her state of mind is what concerned me most. When I confronted her about the changes, she insisted she had actually painted these masterpieces long ago, under pseudonyms. At Schwartz's urging, she decided it was time to put her real name, Angel, on the artwork.

I had lived with my mother for nearly two decades and never once saw her lift a paintbrush, let alone produce a Renaissance portrait or an abstract cubist painting like Picasso. I challenged her claim, but she insisted it was her hand behind every brushstroke. She was offended that I doubted her honesty and her skills. I'd learned over the years you didn't want to be on the receiving end of her wrath, so I backed off.

It's unsettling to catch your parents in a lie. They are your pillars of strength and integrity, the people you can count on for honesty. When they fib, it's a disappointment to find out they are only human, vulnerable to life's pressure like everyone else.

My mom was certainly under stress at this time. Putting the name Angel on the paintings seemed like a twisted way of justifying the turgid praise coming from her new cronies. The scary part was that she believed her own lie.

Her confusion inadvertently resonated in my world, too. Granted, there's a big difference between a young man floundering in his twenties and a middle-age woman lost in menopause. Nonetheless, I saw troubling similarities. Her drug of choice was Valium; I chose pot and coke. Neither of us had fulfilling careers. I started to come around the Milbank house less frequently; it was just too painful.

Gene was still living at home and filled me in on Mom's exploits: dancing the Twist in her spandex hot pants at 3 a.m. on Ventura Boulevard, twenty-four-hour trips with Doctor Gomez to Tijuana to buy cheap prescription drugs, all-night tarot card readings. What a circus.

The person who helped me cope the most during this period was Stan. Having played Chip on *MTS*, Stan was in the unique position of sharing the exact same experiences, in our careers and at home. It was a real blessing to have somebody to commiserate with, and he definitely helped preserve my sanity.

Without steady acting work, I had to do something to keep my creative juices flowing or go crazy. I went back to studying my craft with Jack Garfein. Most of my days were spent rehearsing scenes for his weekly master class. Strindberg, Chekhov, Mamet, Molière, and Arthur Miller were playwrights whose work I loved.

I considered going back to New York to pursue work onstage. Making a permanent move didn't seem like the right thing to do, though. My entire family was in turmoil. The emotional chaos started at the top, with my parents' marital woes, and that filtered down to my younger siblings who were caught in their cross fire. I felt like a rat jumping off a sinking ship, so I stayed put and looked for other acting work. I found it on the dinner theater circuit.

CHAPTER 36

The Poison Donut

 Dinner theaters are all but extinct now, but in the 1970s they were popular in cities all around the country. This type of theater wasn't high art. Dinner theater was a venue where plain folks came to gorge on mediocre buffets and see their favorite TV stars perform live in lowbrow comedies like *Natalie Needs a Nightie* and *See How They Run* (two of my starring vehicles). Hollywood considered such theaters to be the last refuge of has-been stars trying to make an easy buck. I hated to think of it that way, but it was true.

I was offered the lead in Neil Simon's *Star Spangled Girl* at Tiffany's Attic in Salt Lake City. This was about as far from the Great White Way as you could get.

My actor friends counseled me not to do it, fearing I'd damage my sagging reputation. Not likely. I knew my industry standing was already in the toilet, so I accepted the offer to do the play for two months at a thousand dollars per week. It was far better than watching TV and getting high with friends, eating at Taco Bell at 3 a.m., and letting Schwartz read my tarot cards for the umpteenth time. I'd be performing before an audience again. It didn't matter to me if the spectators were socialites from Manhattan or the Mormon Tabernacle Choir. When an audience's laughter washes over, it's a rush. I may have been a has-been, but I wasn't a snob.

Tiffany's Attic in Salt Lake City was a beautiful multitiered dinner theater that seated six hundred people. It was the perfect place for Average Joe America and his wife to eat a meal, down a few drinks, and hopefully have a few laughs. I gave them some unexpected guffaws on opening night when I came very close to dying onstage, literally.

I was playing Norman (another nerd) in the Simon play. In the first act, Norman meets Sophie, a young girl who just moved into his apartment building. It's love at first sight when Sophie introduces herself and gives Norman a cake she just baked. The second she leaves, Norman blabbers to his roommate about Sophie's beauty and her scrumptious cake.

All through rehearsals, things went according to plan: Sophie would enter, say *hi*, hand me a round coffee cake, leave the stage, and then I'd blab.

On opening night, though, the actress playing Sophie entered carrying a different kind of pastry. She handed me a long, shiny glazed donut wrapped in tin foil. It wasn't the round coffee cake in a can that we'd been rehearsing with.

I looked at the strange new pastry in my hand and thought, This is new, I wonder why? Despite the change in props, the show must go on, so I took a bite of the donut and began extolling her wonderful baking skills.

Immediately, I noticed an unmistakable bitterness in my mouth that tasted like a metallic chemical. An alarmed voice went off in my head: *Poison!* A second warning bell sounded: *Spit it out!* Too late.

In my haste to get through my lines, a lump of toxic dough managed to slip past my tongue and enter my esophagus. I started to gag.

My brain issued a new urgent directive: *Get it out of your throat, dummy, before you choke!* Too late, again. The hunk of donut was already lodged in my windpipe, somewhere between my tonsils and my Adam's apple.

Suddenly, the play came to a halt as I stared at my roommate.

I was wordless and gasping. He stared back, wondering why I was not praising Sophie's great baking skills anymore. He also had no idea that I couldn't breathe.

Full-blown panic was welling up inside me. I felt light-headed as my air supply dwindled. I pounded on my back with a clenched fist, trying to dislodge the obstruction, and stumbled around the stage like a dizzy-eyed drunk.

My roommate gaped at my odd behavior, and the audience started to laugh like baboons. Seconds before, I was raving about Sophie's wonderful cake, and now I was gagging on it like it was made of dog shit. It was a brilliant piece of comedy acting . . . had I planned it.

I'd endured about thirty seconds without air and was beginning to see stars. I figured I had two options: run offstage for help or keel over into somebody's plate of mashed potatoes and gravy in the front row. I didn't like either choice. Then another option hit me: use my throat muscles to force the lump downward into my stomach and clear my windpipe.

I attacked the dough ball with my best swallowing effort. My face reddened and my eyes bulged and the crowd thought it was the funniest thing they'd ever seen. They screamed like banshees. With one big grunt, the dough ball finally worked its way around my Adam's apple and slipped down the hatch.

Air! Sweet, sweet oxygen! I could breathe again, but just barely.

I tried to resume expressing my love for Sophie's wonderful baking, but my windpipe collapsed after every other word. Once the larynx has been traumatized, it wants a rest. Unfortunately, I didn't have that luxury; six hundred people were hanging on my every grunt.

I'd eke out a few words of dialogue, then gag, and the audience would convulse with laughter. That was how the scene proceeded until it reached a point where I could exit the stage, which I did to a thundering ovation.

Backstage, I collared the stage manager, Jeff. He was a twenty-year-old drama major from a local college, entrusted to run our production. Jeff's duties included building sets, operating the show's lights and sound, and taking care of props. Normally, these jobs would be divided among a few workers. Tiffany's Attic was on a budget that allowed for only one stagehand. Welcome to the wonderful world of dinner theater.

"What happened to the coffee cake? And what was on that donut?" I gasped, my throat still closing after every word.

Jeff gulped and said, "Just before Sophie was about to go on-stage, she went to the prop table to get the cake, but it wasn't there. She had to give you some kind of pastry in the scene, so I gave her the donut from the third act."

"It tasted horrible, and I choked on it. What was on it?"

He held up a large, yellow spray can of 3M preservative. "The donut wasn't supposed to be eaten. I sprayed it with this, hoping it might last the run of the play."

I grabbed the can and read the warning label: CAN BE FATAL IF SWALLOWED. SEEK HELP IMMEDIATELY IF INGESTED.

Beads of perspiration instantly formed on my forehead. I felt dizzy, and my mind was a blank. Then I heard my roommate's dialogue onstage signaling my cue to reenter. I had no choice but to run back out and continue the play.

Now, back under the glare of the stage lights, I started feeling nauseous. Strange rumblings were going on in my digestive tract, a chemical reaction between my stomach acids and the potent toxins cooked up by the geniuses at 3M. I felt a balloon was inflating my abdomen. I was either going to explode on-stage, like an alien in a science fiction film, or exhale a toxic cloud that would exterminate the first few rows of the audience.

The moment of truth was upon me, and I ran to a window in the apartment set, stuck my head through it, and cut loose with a rolling, thunderous belch. Thank God my expulsion was nothing more than a loud and oddly fragrant burp; it smelled like licorice. Weird.

Once I was certain I wasn't going to project vomit, I pulled my head back through the window and faced my roommate. His face was the picture of befuddlement. My acting partner still had no idea what I was doing or why. His character never goes offstage in the first act, so he never got a chance to ask me or anyone else what was happening.

Toward the end of the act, I heard sirens approaching outside; the 3M warning raced through my mind: "*Can be fatal if swallowed.*" What a lovely headline my demise will make for the tabloids: CHILD ACTOR'S TRAGIC END: POISONED AT A DINNER THEATER. Mercifully, the curtain came down before I keeled over into the audience.

Backstage at intermission, a squad of paramedics greeted me. I thought they'd give me a shot, some kind of antidote, or perhaps put me on pure oxygen. Nope. They gave me a glass of milk.

"Shouldn't I stick my fingers down my throat to induce vomiting and get that poison dough ball out of me?" I asked.

The head paramedic replied, "No! You might get it stuck in your throat. More people die from asphyxiation than from being poisoned."

I understood that completely.

The paramedics huddled, quietly conferring and eyeing me from a distance. After a minute, the head guy came up to me.

"You'll probably be fine," he said. "If you feel any worse later on, go to a hospital." With that sage bit of advice, they packed their gear and left.

I sat there thinking, That's it? They could have told me that on the phone. Why even bother coming?

I finished the play that night without any more belching. There didn't seem to be any ill effects later on, either. From that night on, though, I made it part of my pre-show routine to check the prop table to confirm there were no poisonous pastries.

A newspaper critic who saw the show's opening performance gave us a very favorable review. He singled me out saying: "Barry Livingston has a wonderful control of a variety of expressions and mannerisms." I got a chuckle out of that. In fact, I actually incorporated the choking bit into the rest of my performances. It never approached the crisis level of opening night, but my gagging on Sophie's cake, coupled with my praise for her baking skills, always got a big laugh.

After nearly dying in front of an audience, I've never feared anything going wrong onstage again that I couldn't handle.

CHAPTER 37

The Darkest Hours

I returned to Los Angeles from Salt Lake City and faced two life-changing situations. The first involved my girlfriend, Dale. Our relationship, loving and supportive at first, had run its course. There was no acrimony or drama; we were merely drifting apart. I was leaving town to do theater, and she wanted a more permanent boyfriend. We separated as friends and still are to this day.

The second matter involved my mother's erratic behavior. I tried to keep my distance, but it was impossible to not get sucked in to her bizarre activities. One of the stranger missions: I was recruited to retrieve the discarded dance floor from the Queen Mary. Not the one from the venerable luxury cruise ship. I'm talking about The Queen Mary in Studio City, the infamous gay nightclub.

My mother had noticed that the disco was undergoing a renovation, and the club's old parquet floor was in the trash bins behind the club. According to her psychic cronies, the wood had very good vibes and would look great in her new town house. My parents had just sold our old home on Milbank Street.

I agreed to the covert mission, mainly because my mom and dad were on the verge of getting back together. Kids can never accept their parents' being apart, even if they are like oil and water. I was willing to do everything and anything to keep the peace, even if it meant Dumpster diving for old dance floors.

The plan was for my brothers and I to rendezvous before dawn at the trash bins in the dank alley behind the club. If the coast was clear, we'd pluck the dance floor sections from the garbage and be on our way. Of course, there were risks. The alley behind the club was an infamous pick-up spot for hustlers, male and female. The cops cruised the area regularly, rounding up whomever they could. My fear was that it would be us.

We arrived in the middle of the night, all of us dressed in black like cat burglars. Nothing suspicious about that. No cop cars or hustlers were in sight, so we began our excavation of the smelly, overflowing bins.

I wore the thickest, most industrial rubber gloves I could find and tried hard not to imagine what other treasures of the night I might be touching. The whole stressful time, I could hear a TV newscaster's voice breaking another sad child actor story: *"Barry Livingston on Hard Times: Dumpster Diving Behind a Gay Nightclub."*

My brothers and I selected the least scuffed and warped sections of dance floor, tossed them into my mom's Nova hatchback, and fled from the scene of the crime. Luckily, we didn't get caught.

The dark truth behind Mom's bizarre behavior and emotional turmoil soon revealed itself. She had recently had a momentary blackout while driving and sideswiped a car. This event was impossible to ignore, so she saw a doctor, something my mother rarely did. A week later, after undergoing a battery of tests, she came home after a follow-up meeting with the doctor. My mom stared at me, tears welling, and whispered, "I have cancer."

The initial diagnosis was lung cancer, no doubt from smoking two packs of unfiltered Pall Mall cigarettes a day. More tests revealed that the lung cancer had metastasized to her brain, to her liver, to her kidneys, to just about everywhere in her body. The doctor gave her three months to live. She lasted six.

In her last few months, she and my father made peace with each other. He was a devoted nurse, caring for her until the final days. Anyone who has offered home care in a dire medical situation will know how gut wrenching it can be. My dad rose to the challenge. There was a unique bond between these two flawed human beings. That love revealed itself in the end.

For all my mother's shortcomings, she was a charismatic woman with a bawdy sense of humor and tremendous generosity. She not only raised Stan and me, her biological kids, but she adopted three more children: Bill, Michelle, and Gene. She was also a surrogate mother to dozens of other young people, mainly my friends and those of my siblings. All were welcomed into our home for extended stays. It was her drive and vision that got me into show business, a mixed blessing to be sure. Her aim was true, though. At fifty-five years old, my mother passed away.

I retreated, physically and emotionally, into the sanctuary of my newly purchased house. Dealing with the loss of a parent is always a kick in the gut, no matter how close or distant the relationship was during life. I was very close to my mother, and her loss left a giant hole in my heart. This tragic event, combined with a bleak forecast in acting, led me into the most self-destructive period of my life.

I had a moderate cocaine habit for a couple of years. It was a social thing, partying with friends and using it to impress the girls with the hopes of getting laid, which never happened often enough. Now, I started "freebasing" the drug, purifying the white powder and smoking it. This was the darkest period of my *Lost Weekend*.

I spent many nights getting high until dawn with a drug-dealing buddy, Louie. There's really not much to tell about these events. If you were a fly on the wall watching us, you couldn't have found a duller duo. We'd talk, smoke, talk, cook up a new batch, smoke, talk, talk, talk . . . boring, boring, boring. Eventually, the drug supply would be exhausted and I'd go home.

Like most users who survive the drug, there comes a tipping point, a moment that screams out you are headed for an early grave. Mine occurred late one night while I was trying to score.

It was midweek, about two in the morning, and I kept calling Louie to buy some cocaine. His phone just rang and rang, no answer. I wouldn't give up, though. Anyone who's ever been hooked knows about that crazy need. Finally, at about four in the morning, a raspy, exhausted voice answered the phone.

"What?" Louie hissed.

"Louie, it's Barry. Can I come by?" I purposely left my query vague to throw off any wire-tapping cops. Louie knew the drill.

"Sure, come over," he said. Serious drug dealers run a 24/7 operation and are used to catering to late-night customers.

Minutes later, I skidded to a stop outside Louie's apartment in the Los Feliz area of Los Angeles. It was eerily quiet, nearly dawn. I sprinted to the front door of the building, rang his bell, and waited for a voice on the intercom. I got no answer. I rang again, holding the button down longer than necessary, and waited. Again, nothing. "Shit," I muttered. "He's probably gone back to sleep."

Louie had the upper floor of the old duplex. I noticed that a French door on his balcony was cracked open. I also saw a tall, decorative Conquistador statue nearby; it rose up from the ground floor to right below Louie's balcony, so I decided to play Spider-Man. Proof positive, again, that drugs will make you dumb as a stump.

I hopped up onto the Conquistador's raised, bent knee and climbed. Once I reached his head, I was high enough to pull myself onto the balcony. Ta-dah! Nothing to it! I slipped through the open French door.

Inside Louie's bedroom, I saw my pal sprawled out on his bed, facedown, bare-assed naked and snoring. "Louie," I whispered. He didn't respond. "Loouieeee," I whispered a little louder.

Louie awoke, startled by my voice. In a panic, he whipped out a .38-caliber pistol from under his pillow and aimed at me.

"It's Barry, don't shoot!" I yelled. Too late.

The gun's hammer went *click* . . . but didn't fire.

"What the hell?" said Louie. He stared at his gun and seemed more troubled that his weapon didn't work than the fact he nearly shot me.

"You said to come over; I was downstairs ringing," I yammered.

Louie inspected his weapon and found that it was fully loaded. He grinned and said, "Must've been a bad round. You're a lucky fucker."

I laughed, too, playing along, trying to keep things light. I knew I'd almost had my head blown off, but I didn't want to dwell on that thought. Keeping Louie in a jovial mood, and getting my drugs, was still my main goal. That's how screwed up my priorities had gotten.

I left Louie's house sometime after dawn and went home with my coke, which I finished with one last massive snort.

Once the drug was gone, I tried to sleep. I lay in bed, tossing and turning, unable to turn off my mind. I kept seeing my near-death experience at Louie's. Voices whispered in my head. The most persistent one was my mother who kept repeating: *Stop what you are doing or you will die, goddamn it!*

She loved to swear, even in my dreams.

It'd be too easy to say that my mother's ghostly voice scared me into swearing off drugs. It helped, but frankly, I was already pretty disgusted with my all-night bingeing. My close call with Louie's .38 pushed me into a new level of self-loathing, and I stopped cold-turkey.

My bout with smoking "freebase" lasted six months. Looking back, it felt like years. I never made any solemn vow to quit, no celebrity rehab with Doctor Drew, no big announcement to my friends, no religious conversion. Through a combination of events, I decided to control my addiction and not let it control me.

I say *control* because over the next few years I would have a toot of this or a puff of that if it was offered. Eventually, in a few years, I quit doing everything, period. I was lucky. I heard the saner voices in my head, and summoned the willpower to follow their advice.

Allow me to preach for a moment: drugs are a big waste of time and money, and a threat to everything you should cherish— your passion, your friends, and your life. The best advice I can give kids today, including my own, is don't start down that road.

Unfortunately, teenagers want to know the truth from actual experiences and not from parental words of warning. Fair enough. If you must go there, use extreme caution and moderation. In the end, I hope it won't take a gun pointed at your face to get you to stop. One last thing: listen to the advice of your mother, living or deceased, because she usually knows best.

CHAPTER 38

Staying Sober with John Cassavetes

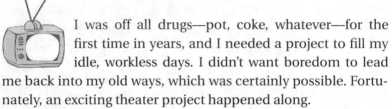 I was off all drugs—pot, coke, whatever—for the first time in years, and I needed a project to fill my idle, workless days. I didn't want boredom to lead me back into my old ways, which was certainly possible. Fortunately, an exciting theater project happened along.

I'd been studying with the brilliant character actor, Martin Landau, who inherited the class of my old mentor, Jack Garfein. One day, completely by chance, the legendary actor/writer/director, John Cassavetes, poked his head into the barren Hollywood warehouse where Landau was conducting classes.

It turned out that Cassavetes hadn't seen Landau since the 1950s when they were both starving actors in New York. Cassavetes said he was looking for a theater space to present three plays he was developing. Landau offered up our empty warehouse and, just like that, Cassavetes accepted. He also asked Landau if he'd like to be a lead in one of the plays. My teacher's acting career in 1980 was almost as dead as mine, so he jumped on the offer, a decision that he came to regret. More on that in a minute.

Cassavetes called the project The Love and Hate Trilogy, and he planned to direct all three plays. The first piece was *Knives,* which Cassavetes had written. Ted Allen wrote the other two plays, *The Third Day Comes* and *Love Streams* (later a Cassavetes film). Gena Rowlands, the director's talented wife, starred in all three plays. Landau was set to do the male lead in *The Third Day Comes,* Jon Voight would costar in *Love Streams,* and Peter Falk headlined *Knives.* Landau's acting class, which I was a member of, became the repertory company that would fill out the supporting roles.

Rehearsals for the plays commenced. At nine in the morning, the cast of *Knives* assembled. The actors would read from the script as Cassavetes paced back and forth, listening. At some point, he'd hear something in the reading, stop the actors mid-scene, and improvise new dialogue. All the while, his assistant would furiously scribble down his verbal riffing. After Cassavetes was done, he'd cackle and signal the actors to continue. At noon, the *Knives* reading concluded and work on *Love Streams* would start with Cassavetes applying the same writing method. At three in the afternoon the cast for *The Third Day Comes* arrived to work with Cassavetes.

The marathon "table reads" and rewrites continued for three weeks. A small forest of trees must have been sacrificed to provide enough paper for the director's improvised revisions. Most of his verbal jamming was brilliant; some of it wasn't. But I was amazed by his stamina, an endless supply of creative energy. I'd heard the rumors about his alcohol and drug abuse, but I never saw it. Perhaps I wasn't looking for it. I was still trying to maintain my new course of sobriety.

In true repertory fashion, the actors lent a hand in the set building process. My job was to sand, stain, and varnish the arms of ninety-nine theater seats. That meant refinishing 198 wooden arms, two per chair, which I did gladly. There was great camaraderie among the company, bonded by our mutual respect for Cassavetes. One actor, though, was becoming increasingly unhappy: Martin Landau.

I was playing the role of a Communist sympathizer in *The Third Day Comes* and privy to Landau's struggle in rehearsals. The play was a *Death of a Salesman* type of a story with Landau portraying a character that was losing his career, his family, and his mind. The role seemed well suited to Landau, but the actor seemed confused and troubled about how to play the character. He'd ask for clarifications about motivations and back story. Cassavetes would chuckle and shrug, leaving his actor ever more frustrated.

As a bystander, I could see that Cassavetes was being purposely vague, hoping that Landau might channel his exasperation into his character's emotional life. They were both method actors after all, well versed in techniques that tap into real feelings.

Landau resisted the Cassavetes approach, and their lines of communication began to fray. Things came to a head one night while rehearsing a scene where Landau's character comes home from work, having just been fired from his longtime job.

Cassavetes said, "Marty, I want you to find a way to enter a scene that suggests you're really losing your mind, okay?" Landau nodded and entered the scene giggling, as if he'd been out getting drunk.

"Stop!" Cassavetes said. "I'm not too sure about the giggling, Marty. Try something different." The actor grimaced. Being a consummate professional, Landau shuffled back offstage. A moment later, Landau entered the scene . . . skipping.

"Hold it, Marty!" John called out again. "Don't skip. Find another way to enter." Landau, tail between his legs, walked off again. This went on for at least five more times: Landau entering in some wacky way and Cassavetes vetoing the choice.

"John, maybe you should come up and show me what you want because I don't know what you want," Landau said, at his wit's end.

Cassavetes was a brilliant actor himself. He leaped at the opportunity and raced up onstage to demonstrate. As Landau looked on, Cassavetes entered, giggling and inebriated, just as Landau had done in his first attempt.

Landau stared, incredulous. "That's exactly what I did twenty minutes ago, the first time!"

Cassavetes cackled as he walked offstage. Landau's bulging eyes were burning a hole in the director's back. John dropped into his chair and said, "Do it like that, Marty, but when you enter I want you to walk in . . . backward." Another cackle.

Landau gawked at John. It looked like he was either going to bolt out the door or choke his tormentor. Being an old-school trouper, though, the actor bit his lip and walked offstage to try to please Cassavetes, again.

The actor made the entrance, this time walking backward and giggling. Oddly enough, it was brilliant; Cassavetes let the scene continue. After it ended, Landau faced Cassavetes and waited for his critique.

Cassavetes grinned and said, "We'll work on it tomorrow."

Not with Landau.

The next day Landau bounded into the theater like a man whose death sentence had just been pardoned by the governor. I asked him what was happening.

His beaming face frowned, and he said, "I'm going to have to bow out of the play."

"Why?"

He kept up a sad veneer, but his twinkling eyes gave him away. "I've just been offered a role in a TV movie, *Death at the Amusement Park*. Mike Connors is the star, but I've got a nice supporting role."

What's a better career move I asked myself: doing *Death at the Amusement Park* with Mike Connors or an original play with Gena Rowland and directed by John Cassavetes? There was already a huge buzz all over Hollywood about John's project; I hadn't heard a thing about the next starring vehicle for Mike Connors. Talk about mixed-up priorities. It was pretty clear: Landau couldn't hack being the director's hand puppet anymore, and this was his ticket out.

Jon Voight's friend, Mike McGuire, took over Landau's role. He jumped into the part with a week of rehearsals and performed his role brilliantly.

Of course, Martin Landau had the last cackle a few years later. His reputation rebounded with the Francis Ford Coppola film, *Tucker: The Man and His Dream,* which earned him an Oscar nomination. After that, he went on to win Oscars for *Ed Wood* and *Crimes and Misdemeanors.* Perhaps doing *Death at the Amusement Park* was a great career move after all.

As opening night approached, we worked around the clock on The Love and Hate Trilogy. Nothing could divert Cassavetes's attention, not even the theft of his car.

I was standing outside the theater and saw two sketchy thugs speed off in the director's blue Dodge. I ran inside to tell him about the theft, expecting him to express shock or dismay. Instead, he cackled, as usual.

"Shouldn't we call the cops?" I asked.

"Why bother?" he said.

"Huh?" I replied.

"It's a rental car," he said with a shrug. "I haven't the faintest idea where I got it. I can't even remember how long I've had it! Sooner or later somebody will get in touch." Then, he went back to work.

The Love and Hate Trilogy opened, and, in typical Cassavetes fashion, some critics hated the plays, calling them boring and self-indulgent, and others loved them for their unique characters and intense acting moments. I had lost all objectivity. I was just glad to have been there to witness the crazy worlds that Cassavetes orchestrated onstage and off. He was a true maverick.

CHAPTER 39

Finding My Soul Mate
During CPR

Working on the plays fulfilled my artistic needs and helped stifle my drug cravings. That was important. There was still a big, painful hole in my life that was missing: a meaningful relationship. I'd troll the pick-up bars or go to the local gym to ogle the pretty girls, but I never met anyone I really liked. One night at the Red Onion Restaurant and Cantina in Canoga Park, I got lucky. My life was changed forever.

I was seated at the crowded bar, nursing a drink and trying to tune out a bad country western band playing onstage. The film, *Urban Cowboy*, was a recent hit and most every nightclub in town had ditched the *Saturday Night Fever* disco ball for sawdust floors.

A pretty young girl sat down next to me. I don't remember who started the conversation, but the next thing I knew we were chatting; actually, it was more like yelling over the pounding drums and whining guitars. I learned that her name was Karen and suggested we go somewhere else to talk.

Moments later we were outside the club, and things took an unexpected and tragic turn. I noticed a young woman lying flat on her back on a grassy knoll. People were hurrying to and from the club, completely ignoring her. I thought I might score a few chivalrous points with Karen and suggested that we should see if the girl was okay.

As we drew closer, I could see that the girl's white dress had a floral pattern on it, red roses, I thought.

Once we were standing over her, I realized the red pattern was actually large bloody stains. The girl was motionless, and her upturned wrist was severely slashed. It was a gruesome sight, and I went light-headed, nearly passing out.

Karen was studying to be a physical therapist in college and had some medical training. She sprung into action, using her sweater to tie a tourniquet around the bloody wrist. The girl had a pulse but was not breathing, so Karen started to administer CPR. Between blowing puffs of air into the woman's slack-jawed mouth, Karen yelled, "Call an ambulance!"

For those of you old enough to remember, there were no cell phones in 1980. You couldn't just whip out a Motorola and dial for help. In fact, there wasn't even the universal emergency number, 911, to call. My only option was to run back inside the Red Onion and seek medical assistance.

I plowed through the line of people waiting to get inside the nightclub, all the while yelling, "Emergency, this is an emergency, let me through!" I finally arrived at the velvet rope and a hulking doorman.

"There's a young girl bleeding to death on your front lawn," I yelled, trying to be heard over the loud music that was spilling out of the club.

"My front . . . what?" the doorman asked, giving me a confused look.

I realized that I had to slow down and carefully explain the situation or the poor girl was never going to survive. "There's a girl who is lying out by the street, on the front lawn of your club. She needs a doctor and an ambulance because she is bleeding to death!" I said emphatically.

The doorman finally got it. He picked up an in-house phone and reported the problem to management. A long minute later, a club employee appeared onstage and commandeered the microphone. He put forth the famous question: "Is there a doctor in the house? Would a doctor please come to the front door immediately?" It's a wonder that anybody survived a medical crisis back then.

Seconds later a doctor appeared at the door, and I led him back to the lawn where Karen was still doing CPR. When the man announced that he was a doctor, Karen jumped away from the girl, ready and relieved to hand over the trauma. To Karen's credit, the girl was now breathing on her own again.

An ambulance soon arrived, and paramedics joined the team. They said she was going to survive thanks to our actions. The police arrived, too. Since Karen and I were the ones who found her, the cops told us not to leave because a report had to be taken. What a swell Saturday night this was turning into.

Eventually, the ambulance sped away with the girl, and a droll policeman interviewed Karen and me. We had nothing to offer about the girl or her suicide attempt, since we had found her unconscious. Nonetheless, the Jack Webb clone meticulously assembled the facts, some of them I found quite interesting. I learned that Karen grew up in Walnut Creek, California, and her age was twenty-one. These were the kinds of things that guys pry out of girls over time. Kudos to the LAPD for their excellent investigation.

The police released us, and we went to Karen's nearby apartment where we bonded in a comforting and profound embrace . . . one that's lasted thirty years.

In our first twenty-four hours, Karen and I saved somebody's life, became lovers, and went to Disneyland for an outing with my entire family—siblings, cousins, aunts, and uncles. What a whirlwind.

I had never been more instantly enraptured with anybody. Karen was as beautiful as she was smart. She laughed at all my silly jokes, and I laughed at hers. We got each other, simple as that. I had found my soul mate and soon we were married.

CHAPTER 40

The Worst and the Best

With a new love buoying my spirit, I threw myself into a number of theater productions in Los Angeles. The first one was a musical, *Purple Hearts and Other Colors,* about the World War II invasion of Iwo Jima. It was perhaps the most ill-conceived song and dance epic since *Springtime for Hitler,* and featured show-stopping numbers like "We Need a Negro Too." Sondheim, eat your heart out.

The musical was based on an old screenplay written by Robert C. Jones, an Academy Award winner for his work on the film *Coming Home.* To be fair to Mr. Jones, screenplays rarely transfer well to theater. When a script written for a movie describes a battleship's blazing guns, landing crafts streaking ashore, and thousands of troops pouring onto exploding tropical beaches, it can work like gangbusters on screen, especially on a 200-million-dollar budget. When you're trying to dramatize the same mind-boggling action on a minuscule stage, with a few hundred dollars to spend, the spectacle is, shall I say, diminished.

At the Beverly Hills Playhouse, we had ten Japanese soldiers hunkered down on the left side of the stage and ten American G.I.'s (including me . . . and the Negro from the song) clumped together on the right side. As the action progressed, we inched (literally) toward each other, pausing occasionally to break out into song and dance.

In the end, my pacifist Negro pal dies tragically in my arms, and a similar senseless fate befalls his Japanese counterpart. There wasn't a dry eye in the house, mainly because everybody left at intermission.

I approached my role, the Innocent Midwestern Kid, like Olivier preparing to do Hamlet. Frankly, I was happy to be working and had convinced myself that we were on the verge of making theatrical history. I even asked Karen to bring her parents, Ben and Nancy, to see me work. When Karen announced our engagement a short time later, it's no small wonder they warned her: "Are you sure you want to marry an actor?"

Once we opened and the incredulous reviews were in, I saw the musical in a new light. We approached it as a drama, a serious statement about the "madness of war." It should have been comedy, which it was, unintentionally.

My only defense: I was just the actor, I didn't write this shit.

I followed up *Purple Hearts,* easily my worst play, with a theater piece that ranks as my best. Talk about a creative whiplash.

The play was called *Creeps,* a story about four men afflicted with cerebral palsy who are living at a run-down institution. The spirit of the play is similar to the story of the Elephant Man. It depicts people with CP as intelligent and sensitive, normal in every way except for their contorted speech and appearance. Because of these external burdens, they find themselves ostracized by society.

The play's theme resonated with me. I knew what it felt like to be shunned, too, having been labeled (unfairly in my mind) as a has-been. Granted, being spurned by Hollywood was a minor offense compared to the rejection that people with CP experience. Still, as an actor, I found an emotional connection.

The play's director, Jeff Murray, accompanied me to an L.A. county facility, a home for people with CP, to study physical and speech impediments. One woman in particular, Karen Dick, became a role model for my character. Her handicaps, contorted limbs and strangled speech, would have driven the average normal person to consider ending their lives. Not Karen, though. She faced every obstacle with courageous determination and self-effacing humor. Eventually, she left the institution, got a job, and even bought a home. Karen Dick is a winner and inspired me to never give up, never let other people define who you really are.

During the fourteen-month run at Theatre Theater in 1983, the play was a huge critical hit and won numerous awards. The work I did in *Creeps* was an artistic highlight. It made me grow as an actor. Perhaps more important, playing a person with CP made me reevaluate the rejection I was feeling in my own life. It became clear that you either succumb to your condition or you face it head on and conquer it, no matter what the outside world thinks about you. It's a matter of heart over mind.

CHAPTER 41

Wanted, Again

In the 1980s, my focus was on theater because that's the only place I could practice my craft. The eight-year drought in TV that began in 1975 ended when I was cast in a TV movie, *High School, U.S.A.* Ironically, the cast was a hodgepodge of ex–child stars (me, Tony Dow, Todd Bridges, Elinor Donahue, etc. . . .) playing teachers and TV's current child stars (Michael J. Fox, Crispin Glover, Nancy McKeon) were the students. It was high concept at its tackiest.

Michael J. Fox was the hottest young actor on the tube at that time. He seemed cocky as hell, too, oblivious to how fickle youthful fame can be. I couldn't resist reminding him of this fact during a cast publicity photo. He was kneeling in front of me, Jerry Mathers and Frank Bank (both from *Leave It to Beaver*) and Bob Denver and Dwayne Hickman (both from *Dobie Gillis*). I tapped Michael on the shoulder, drawing his attention to the motley crew standing right behind him. I whispered in a gleeful, ghostly voice: "We'll be waiting for you."

Michael snorted sarcastically. "Yeah, sure." Lucky for him, he was about to start work on *Back to the Future*. That mega-hit franchise launched his film career. He could have just as easily joined our ranks. You never know.

I followed the TV movie with guest spots on a couple of hit TV shows, *Simon & Simon* and *Hart to Hart*. Out of nowhere, things started looking up. The film industry is such a crazy, unpredictable business that it's hard to say what might have precipitated this mini-revival. A few things come to mind.

I was drug free and in love. Both things really lifted my spirits. Nobody wants to hire a slug. I was also hungrier for work than ever before. I had reached a point where it bugged the hell out of me that I could be dismissed by the industry so summarily. That stoked a fire in my gut, and I prepared for every audition like it was my last. My readings couldn't be merely good; they had to be amazing. I had to blow the producers away so they would have no choice but to give me the role. That's what I aimed for anyway.

I was on a roll, again, and got a nice supporting part in a major feature film, *Masters of the Universe.*

The *Star Wars* franchise was the envy of every studio for the millions of movie tickets it sold. More than that, the film's characters were an ongoing, bottomless gold mine in the toy market. Every producer was hungry for a taste of the merchandising bonanza that followed a hit sci-fi film.

In the case of *Masters,* the studio was going to try something different: make a movie based on an existing line of action figures. Mattel Toys had already built the *Masters* toy line into a worldwide phenomenon. Every little boy under fourteen had He-Man, the hero, and Skeletor, the villain. In today's parlance, the franchise was already a *brand name* and seemed like a slam-dunk at the box office.

The Swedish hulk, Dolph Lundgren, was hired to play He-Man opposite the brilliant actor, Frank Langella, as Skeletor. I was a mere earthling, Charlie, whose record store is demolished when the hero and villain do battle in my shop. Rounding out the cast was Courtney Cox (years before *Friends*), Billy Barty, and Christina Pickles, among others. The accountants were already counting the profits as production on the film began. They never foresaw the nightmares involved in making the movie.

Dolph Lundgren was an amazing physical specimen, perfect for He-Man, but was barely intelligible when acting. Example: He-Man would enter a scene and exclaim, "Grab Gwildor! (Billy Barty). Skeletor's men are coming!" In rehearsals, Lundgren's words were fairly clear. He wasn't Richard Burton doing Hamlet, but it was passable English. Once the director yelled *action*, though, He-Man's adrenaline kicked in and the words came out as: "Graeeeb, Gweeeelda! Skaaaalatooor's mans ahhhrrrr kaaaaming!" Lundren was emoting in a language of his own making.

Apart from the fact that the star couldn't be understood, a serious flaw, there were other production problems. The plan was to start shooting every night around eight o'clock, using downtown Whittier, California, as our main location. Most nights shooting for the first scene began at three in the morning, *seven hours* after our scheduled start. Why? I honestly don't know.

An actor is supposed to get into wardrobe, put on makeup, do a rehearsal for the camera people, and wait for the crew to set up lights. Once that's done, the actors are called to the set to start filming. If the scene is complicated (car chases, explosions, dancing girls), it can take an hour, sometimes two, to go from camera rehearsal to filming. On *Masters*, even the simplest of scenes, say two actors sitting on a bench talking, required endless hours to set up.

Meanwhile, the actors would sit around, shooting the shit, playing cards, reading the newspapers or, in some cases, doing drugs to keep awake. I was playing an earthling and spared the grief of having to sit around in some crazy alien makeup. Poor Frank Langella wasn't so lucky, though. His entire head was encased in heavy prosthetic Skeletor makeup.

Every night Langella arrived at our location two hours before the other actors so the makeup artists could slather his face with layers of gooey latex. The goop would then harden into a rubber skull mask and was claustrophobic as hell. Making things even more miserable for Langella, he could only eat liquid meals ingested through a straw, so as not to ruin the makeup.

Langella got so fed up with the routine of sitting around in full makeup every night for nine to ten hours, he eventually snapped. In a claustrophobic fit, he ripped at the layers of latex coating his face, yelling obscenities. Of course, the moment his face was finally freed, an assistant said they were ready to shoot his scene. With bits of rubber dangling from his nose and ears, Langella screamed, "Screw it. I'm going home!" And he did. The production of *Masters* seemed cursed with such moments.

After weeks of filming, the movie was far behind schedule and way over budget. Cannon Films (the producing company) was on the brink of bankruptcy, completely out of money, and stopped production before the film was completed. The Mattel Toy Company, having a keen interest in the film's success, coughed up a few more bucks to shoot the final scene, a climactic fight between He-Man and Skeletor. For anyone who saw the movie, you might think that the battle was shot in a big dark box. It was. Mattel didn't pony up very much dough.

Eventually, the film was released and sank like a brick at the box office. So much time had elapsed between the first day of filming and the premiere, the popularity of the He-Man craze had faded. Kids, ever the fickle consumers, had moved on to the next phenomenon: *Transformers*. My hopes of having an action figure made in my character's image were history.

CHAPTER 42

Unwanted, Again

 Just when I thought my career was out of the woods, another dark forest loomed in front of me. Film and TV work disappeared, again. This was a discouraging development, enough to drive a normal person insane, but I had seen a few ebbs and flows in my life by now. I didn't like being out of work, but I could handle it.

Luckily, I had a support group to help keep me positive. I could commiserate with my pals, other talented artists like Steve Railsback, Robert Hummer, Alex Rocco, and my screenwriter pal, Brent Maddock, who would soon write the sci-fi film classic, *Tremors*. I also had my brother Stan who was fighting the exact same career windmills as me.

Most important, I had Karen. She was completely unimpressed by the glitz associated with actors. The highs and lows of my career were secondary to being a good husband and person. Thanks to her unconditional love, I began to separate my self-worth as a person from my worth as an actor in Hollywood. I still cared deeply about my career, but I also saw that I had another life to live besides acting. The trick was to get *both* things, home life and career, to flourish at the same time. I'd have to come up with another new plan to conquer Everest.

A wise, obviously unemployed actor once said, "The real job of an actor is the time spent looking for work, not the time spent acting." I took that dictum to heart, sending out flyers to industry people to notify them of my plays, writing thank-you letters to anyone who'd give me an audition, and scouring the trade papers to keep tabs on upcoming projects, particularly if they were being developed by producers and directors I had worked for previously. Nothing much came out of this effort, but it did fill my days with purpose.

One of my other favorite activities was to drop in on former employers, directors like Richard Donner or Randal Kleiser, hoping to jog their memory and let them know that I was still alive. This was important, especially since I'd heard rumors that some fans thought I'd died in Vietnam!

Of course, meeting face to face with the industry elite meant getting past the surly guards who manned the gates at every studio. Once again, the walled compounds of Paramount, Universal, and 20th Century-Fox seemed like the impenetrable "forts" of my childhood. I had to be sneaky to gain access.

Warner Bros. in Burbank was my favorite studio for unsanctioned visits. I discovered an unlocked doorway at the outer wall near the main entrance. I'd loiter at the curb out by the street, waiting for three or four cars to line up at the gate. When the guards were busy checking identities, I'd casually slip through the doorway like a cat burglar. This system worked perfectly for months. Then, one day, a guard spotted me.

"Hey, you! Come here!" a uniformed man yelled.

I couldn't bear the thought of being ejected by the goon. Running away seemed pretty humiliating, too, so I dashed through my secret entrance.

Once I was inside, I ran to a ladder attached to a building and climbed like a monkey on speed. Seconds later, three guards blasted through the door. My only option was to freeze, about halfway up the ladder. Thank God, they didn't look up.

The goon squad dashed down the studio corridor, assuming they were hot on my trail. I continued my climb and hid on the roof for forty-five minutes. The whole time, I kept visualizing another news flash: *"Unemployed Ex–Child Actor Caught Stalking the Stars at Warner Bros.!"*

Once I got past the imagined shame, the charade was pretty exciting, and I climbed off the rooftop and continued on my trek around the lot. The guards must not have gotten a good look at my face because I crossed their paths a couple of times. I acted like I was some studio bigwig contemplating a deal and marched past them. As long as you looked like you belonged, nobody bothered you.

The next time I visited the Warner Bros. lot (officially invited for a job audition) I noticed that my secret passage had a padlock on it. Bummer. I wasn't deterred from my mission of prowling the studio, though. You never knew whom you'd bump into. One day, I had an unexpected encounter with Steven Spielberg.

I had just auditioned for a role in *The Waltons* (didn't get it) and bumped into a man named William Fraker. He had been a camera assistant many years ago when I was working on *The Adventures of Ozzie and Harriet.* In the intervening decades, he had moved up in the world and was now Steven Spielberg's cinematographer on *1941,* the director's highly anticipated follow-up to *Jaws.* Fraker grabbed me by the arm and said I must come meet Steven. I didn't protest.

To my amazement, Spielberg practically leaped out of his director's chair to shake my hand. *My Three Sons* was one of his favorite shows as a kid, and Ernie Douglas was a character he strongly related to.

The next thing I know, Spielberg's got me by the arm, dragging me over to meet Amy Irving (his future first wife) and John Belushi (he couldn't have cared less). Spielberg then instructed me to stand with him next to the camera so I could watch the action. We parted ways with a friendly handshake. This was a very good day; perhaps the start of what could be a fruitful relationship. Things always seem to change, though.

Fast-forward five years, not long after *E.T.,* Spielberg's next phenomenal success. I was at Warner Bros. once again, and I met a friend who was working on the director's next film, *Twi-light Zone: The Movie*. My buddy called a higher-up on the film and got permission for me to enter the set, which was strictly off limits to visitors. The studio was guarding the secrets of the script, and Spielberg. Since I had seen him last, he had gradu-ated from "boy wonder" to "film-making genius" and was the most valuable commodity in Hollywood.

I entered the cavernous stage and stood on the sidelines, watching Spielberg set up a shot. At last he glanced over at me, and I waved to him. I was expecting a replay of our first meeting: Steven welcoming me with a bear hug, ushering me around the set to meet the stars.

Instead, the director gave me an odd, puzzled stare, like he was thinking: Who the hell is that and how did he get in here? I watched him work for a few more minutes and realized he wasn't coming over to say *hi*.

Since Spielberg is a bona fide filmmaking genius, I'll give him the benefit of the doubt and assume I was interrupting his con-centration on his work. One way or the other, it felt like I was getting the cold shoulder, so I decided to leave before I was asked to do so.

CHAPTER 43

Back to the Dinner Theater

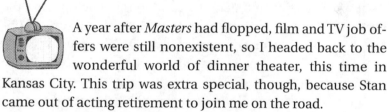 A year after *Masters* had flopped, film and TV job offers were still nonexistent, so I headed back to the wonderful world of dinner theater, this time in Kansas City. This trip was extra special, though, because Stan came out of acting retirement to join me on the road.

The first play we performed together was *See How They Run* at Tiffany's Attic in K.C. On the surface, Tiffany's theater looked quite impressive with massive chandeliers, red-flocked walls, and comfy leather booths on four tiers. Peek behind the curtain, though, and it had a serious problem: roaches.

Anytime food was prepared and served in mass quantities, the little buggers could come running. One night, right in the middle of the play, I heard troubled voices whispering in the front row. I kept my focus on Stan, trying to stay in the scene, but out of the corner of my eye I saw a man slapping the stage with his shoe. The audience roared as a roach, big as a Cadillac, ran back and forth trying to avoid the shoe's crushing blow.

Judging by the crowd's response, it seemed as if they were used to such spectacles, perhaps even looking forward to them. A collective *Ahhhh!* rang out once the bug was finally flattened. The focus then returned to the actors, and we continued on with the play. Talk about being upstaged.

Another night, the theater's roof leaked during a tremendous

Midwestern rainstorm, and steady streams of water dripped down onto the stage. The audience wasn't getting wet, so the management decided the show must go on. Only the actors were getting drenched.

As the play progressed, so did the storm outside. One of the waterfalls pouring down from the ceiling was landing on a bed onstage, a focal point of the play, a farce called *Little White Lies.* Throughout the action, babies kept showing up on my doorstep and I would hide them in the bed. Every time I'd stuff a new baby (dolls, in reality) into the rain-soaked bed, the audience exploded with snickering laughter.

In the play's final moment, I was supposed to climb into the sack with the babies. Up to that point, I refrained from ad libbing about the rain on strict orders from the stage manager. He was afraid that if I acknowledged the theater's leaky roof, the audience might want refunds.

The second I crawled into the soaking bed, the crowd laughed again. They had watched the downpour all evening and knew how wet it was. I couldn't resist a final ad lib and yelled, "Ohmigod! These babies pissed everywhere!" The audience went wild. Our rain-soaked efforts were rewarded with a standing ovation that night.

CHAPTER 44

New Roles

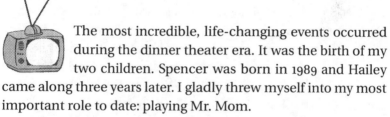 The most incredible, life-changing events occurred during the dinner theater era. It was the birth of my two children. Spencer was born in 1989 and Hailey came along three years later. I gladly threw myself into my most important role to date: playing Mr. Mom.

While Karen was bringing home the bacon working as a physical therapist, I was in charge of packing lunches, taking the kids to school, picking them up, and playing with them in the afternoon. If we weren't at the zoo or museums, we'd be home making up imaginary games.

Being an actor, I loved to play Cheetah the Chimp to Spencer's Tarzan or give a voice to Ken while Hailey pretended to be Barbie. In a traditional marriage, dads work all day at the office and miss their children's wonder years. Not me. I had a blast. It meant revisiting all the things I loved doing as a kid with my own children.

Being a father had an unexpected impact on my career, too. It made me want to work even harder to hot-wire my inert career. Call it pride or ego, but I wanted them to be proud of their dad. At the very least, I wanted them to see me fighting for something.

I intensified my campaign to reintroduce myself to casting directors and producers with a barrage of letters inviting them to see me in my stage productions: *Grease* (produced by Fran

Drescher), *The Last Good Word, Very Cherry and Extra Clean* at the Cast Theatre in Hollywood, and the American premiere of *Cause Célèbre* at the Ahmanson Theatre.

I also took a screenwriting class at UCLA in the evening, hoping to sell a script that would have an acting role for me in it. It worked for Sylvester Stallone in *Rocky* when nobody else would hire him.

The script that came out of my class was titled *Blessing in Disguise.* To my amazement, it won an award in a university competition, the Diane Thomas Screenwriting Awards. Michael Douglas, Danny DeVito, and Steven Spielberg sponsored the contest, so it elicited a huge number of script submissions.

DeVito was the presenter at the awards ceremony. When my name was called, it created quite a buzz among the reporters who recognized me from *MTS.* They were eager for any angle to hype this low-key ceremony. Camera crews from *Entertainment Tonight* swarmed me the minute I stepped off the podium with my award.

Once things settled down, DeVito sidled up next to me and covertly whispered, "Congratulations on the award but . . . who the hell are you anyway?" He confessed to not being a fan of the show.

Suddenly, I possessed an award-winning script; I thought the industry would snap it up. Didn't happen. The script was universally rejected because the subject matter involved a Hollywood bugaboo: old people. The story focused on three senior citizens living at a retirement villa who start a detective agency, using the old folks home and their geezer qualities as their cover. It was *CSI* meets *The Golden Girls;* not the best idea ever conceived but certainly as good as *My Mother the Car.*

Between taking care of the kids and acting in plays, I cranked out scripts with the help of my Remington electric typewriter and gallons of Wite-Out. I didn't sell anything (until years later), but it kept me busy. If writing, acting, and child rearing weren't enough, I decided to try out another title: director.

A playwright friend named Michael Farkash had written a play titled *Meat Dreams*. I found it to be perverse, sexy, and original. Perfect. Plans were made to stage the piece on the off nights (Monday through Wednesday) at a theater in Century City. This was the fiefdom of a man I'll call Ivan Cohen, the most unscrupulous theater producer in Los Angeles, a fact I wish I'd known before signing the contract.

At first glance, Ivan the Terrible (a nickname we gave him) struck you as a typical old-school hippie: owner of a rusty VW bus, tattered blue jeans, and a long gray, bushy beard. His Grateful Dead T-shirts and love beads suggested that he was a love child, full of peace and understanding.

I soon learned that Ivan was petty, loutish, and flat-out dishonest. He probably worked for Dow Chemicals in the 1960s and hated "flower children." Whatever. Ivan told me that *Meat Dreams* would have a budget of one hundred bucks and, oh yeah, we'd have to provide our own toilet paper. Now that's *cheap*, I remember thinking. Our first production meeting ended with my producer saying, "You're sure you really want to direct this piece of shit?" Not exactly a confidence-building pep talk.

Rehearsals commenced, and we worked in the garage of my house, mainly because Ivan wouldn't let us use his theater. Apparently, he needed every spare minute to polish up his long-running hit, *Bleacher Bums*. It was playing on weekends at the theater, and a gala re-opening of *Bums* was in the works. We'd have to rehearse our little "piece of shit" elsewhere.

As fate would have it, *Meat Dreams* premiered in the same week that Ivan's *Bleacher Bums* re-opened. The *Los Angeles Times* printed the reviews of the two plays, side-by-side. *Bums* was savaged by the critics while *Meat Dreams* got a rave review written by the esteemed theater critic Robert Koehler. Ah! Sweet revenge!

On the strength of more good reviews, *Meat Dreams* became a cultish hit and drew large audiences. People barely go to the theater in Los Angeles under the best of circumstances, let alone on a Monday or Tuesday. Smelling money, Ivan decided to move our show to his other, larger theater, so we could perform on the weekends. It was great that more people would see our hard work, but the move also had a big downside: we'd be closer to Ivan's office and his intrusive reach.

Tensions were already high as we switched venues. For months at the Century City Playhouse, we'd coped with Ivan's faulty sound and lighting equipment, his negligence in paying the actors, and of course, the TP issue. As long as the integrity of our show wasn't horribly compromised onstage, we coexisted. Now that we were under Ivan's close supervision, my worst fears came true and our relationship exploded.

Neither of Ivan's theaters had air-conditioning. It's a luxury that few small theaters can afford, and the audiences who attend such venues understand this fact. They'll accept a modest amount of discomfort in exchange for challenging theater. For some reason, Ivan decided to address the temperature problems on our second opening night. He installed six ancient, rattling, oscillating fans in the room where the play was being performed. The fans didn't do a damn thing to cool the room and created a clacking, rattling racket.

Gene Butler, the lead actor in our show, alerted me to the problem about ten minutes before the audience was admitted. I walked into the theater and was stunned by the noise. It sounded like a squadron of Sopwith Camel airplanes from World War I had started up their propeller engines and were preparing to take off.

Ask any stage veteran, and they'll tell you that a theater space should be as quiet as a church because silence can be as compelling as the author's words. In Ivan's theater, our words and silences were going to be buried under a wheezing, whirring din. This crossed the line in terms of protecting the play's integrity, and I wasn't about to let that happen.

I hunted for Ivan and found him in his office, counting the money from the evening's admissions. I made a passionate plea for him to turn off the fans and pointed out that it wasn't even that hot.

He barely looked up from his pile of dough and grumbled, "I got a good deal on the fans at a swap meet. We'll be using them from now on."

Ivan owned the theater and had the right to change things as he saw fit. Fair enough. What really got under my skin was his instantaneous dismissal of my concerns. I'd tolerated his bullshit for months, and I'd finally reached my overload point. Sewer workers call this "blowback time," when a holding tank can't take any more pressure and the shit literally comes flying out the open pipes. Ivan was about to get blasted.

"Either the fans are turned off or the performance is canceled," I snarled. This got his attention.

"Nobody cancels a performance in my theater, except me!" he bellowed.

"It's *our* play and we *will* cancel the performance if the fans stay on. All of that clacking and whirring white noise is going to ruin the show! What's the fucking point?"

"The point is that the audience has already paid for the show!" he said, pointing to the piles of cash on his messy desk.

"Then you'll have to give it back!" I yelled, and dashed out of his office.

I marched into the theater and stood before the chattering audience, waving my hands to get their attention. I said, "Due to technical difficulties, tonight's show is canceled. I'm very, very sorry."

Ivan burst into the room and began screaming, "The show isn't canceled! This show is not canceled!"

I yelled over his voice, "Tonight's performance *is* canceled, and you should see Ivan for a refund." Hearing that, Ivan's eyes bugged out of his head like a Warner Bros. cartoon character. I rushed outside rather than continue the debate in front of the confused spectators.

I paced outside the theater's door, trembling, trying to regain my composure. I heard Ivan's panicked voice still yelling, "The show is not canceled. It is not canceled! Nobody move! I'll be right back!"

Ivan burst through the theater's door, and we went nose to nose, like a couple of WWF wrestlers.

"Give the audience their money, Ivan!" I said.

"I won't give it back!"

"Turn off the fans then!"

"Don't tell me what to do!"

"Turn off the *fans!*"

"*I'll call the union on you!*" he threatened. "*This is my theater! You can't tell me what to do!*"

I repeated, "*Turn off the* fans! *Turn off the* fans! *Turn off the goddam* fans, *Ivannnnn!*" Every time the word *fans* exploded from my mouth, I leaped into the air like an enraged chimp, levitating on adrenaline and anger.

Ivan abruptly fell silent, and his neck puffed up from the venomous words being choked back. I wasn't sure what was coming next. Either he was going to punch me in the nose or I was going to rip his smelly Grateful Dead T-shirt off his back. He turned away and stomped back inside the theater.

I stood there wondering, What the hell is this lunatic doing now?

Moments later, Ivan blasted back out the theater door and hissed, "I'm leaving one small fan on. Just *one!*"

The thought crossed my mind to go "all or nothing." I was still damned steamed. Before firing back, though, I glanced over at Gene Butler and the other actors in the show. They were huddled together in costume, torn between supporting me and wanting to perform that night. I also thought of the audience who had schlepped down to Ivan's theater, only to have their evening ruined by our amateur theatrics. A compromise seemed the only sensible thing to do. I acquiesced to Ivan's one rattling fan.

The play went on that night, and the performance was one of

the best. Ivan disappeared for the next few days, resurfacing when our next good reviews hit the press. He offered up a conciliatory handshake, and I accepted it. My mouth dropped, though, when he asked me to direct another play for him. This was an offer that only a masochist could embrace. I declined.

It may sound strange, but I've come to believe that my confrontation with Ivan marked a cosmic turning point in my life. Cosmic? I know, stay with me. When I was protesting the fans, in essence yelling *I'm mad as hell and I'm not going to take it anymore!* I was finally taking a bold stand and bellowing my righteous indignation. My rage against *windmills,* or fans, finally got the attention of the gods, and my luck changed dramatically.

CHAPTER 45

A Brave New Nerd

 I was asked to audition for a new kind of role, an authority figure. The part was Doctor Rickett on the hit TV show *Doogie Howser, M.D.* This was a first. I had spent my entire professional life playing nerds: the child nerd next door, the teen nerd at college, the twenty-something nerd who can never get laid after college, the middle-aged nerd whose record store gets blown up by Skeletor. I was always the clueless goofball asking all the dumb questions. Finally, I had a shot at portraying an authority figure, the guy who has all the right answers. I read for the producer, Steven Bochco, and got the part. One small role for Mr. Bochco, one giant leap in Barry's career.

To be honest, the role of Doctor Rickett wasn't all that pivotal in the storylines. My job was to blow into a patient's room, make a diagnosis, and educate young Doogie with tongue-twisting medical terms. Not every actor can rattle off this kind of complicated verbiage and make it sound as easy as reciting a grocery list. I could. Casting directors could now envision me in a whole new vista of mature roles: doctors, lawyers, and professors. I fit the description of a cutting-edge 1990s prototype: the yuppie (young, urban professional).

Ironically, there was another factor that made me seem more mature and professional, something that I'd been fighting for years: hair loss. Talk about a blessing in disguise. The more hair that fell out, the more I began to work. That may seem like a silly way to account for my new image, but it's a pretty silly business. In my mind, the hair-loss theory is just as valid as my cosmic fan thesis. Take your pick.

I noticed another shift in my universe while working on *Doogie Howser:* the younger actors treated me like the "old pro." Suddenly, people wanted to hear stories about my days working at Desilu, MGM, and Paramount when I was a kid. It felt good, like the circle was completing itself. I was becoming William Frawley! Okay, maybe Roddy McDowall.

I even passed along Roddy's advice to a young Neil Patrick Harris: *If you want to make it as an adult actor, go to New York and learn your craft onstage.* Harris, in fact, did exactly that and had a big career breakthrough on Broadway with the musical *Rent.* I'm not trying to take credit for his success. He's earned every adult accolade on his own. Then again, who knows? Maybe my words, courtesy of Roddy, stuck. If I ever run into Harris, I'll have to ask.

After finishing *Doogie,* I played another medic, this time acting as O.J. Simpson's doctor in a TV movie, *The O.J. Simpson Story.* The one amazing thing about this Fox project is we started shooting *one week* after O.J.'s famous Ford Bronco "slow speed pursuit." The script was literally written on the fly, ripped from the daily headlines as the Simpson story unfolded.

Now that I had two doctor roles on my résumé I branched out into the legal profession with a recurring attorney role on the TV series, *Lois & Clark: The New Adventures of Superman.* I played Sheldon Bender, the unscrupulous consigliere for Lex Luthor. This role added a new dimension to my widening list of characters. It was my first adult "bad guy."

One of the show's producers, Paul Jackson, told me an interesting story about how I won the role. My job interview was being held in the office of the series show-runner, Robert Singer. Right in the middle of my scene, a long-winded monologue, a telephone rang in the room and Singer answered it.

Now I was in a pickle and had a choice to make: do I stop reading because the executive producer, the man who might hire me, is ignoring my performance, or do I press on, ignoring the slight? Believe it or not, the latter option is the smart choice and that's what I did, even though I was secretly irritated as hell.

I finished my monologue just as Singer concluded his phone conversation. He uttered the typical critique, *Thanks for coming*, and I left the room, crestfallen. My shot at a terrific "bad guy" role was blown by a phone call . . . or so I thought.

Jackson told me later, after we'd become friends, that the call was from the studio head, Les Moonves, and Singer had to take it. My buddy also confided Singer's assessment of my talent: "If Barry is that good during a phone conversation, he's good enough to hire."

I really was becoming the "old pro."

CHAPTER 46

My Dad

 On the home front, my dad moved in with my family. He was eighty years old and ailing with Parkinson's, emphysema, and congestive heart failure. This did not prevent him from driving to Las Vegas whenever the mood struck him, which was often. We feared for his safety, as well as the other drivers on the road, but a parent rarely heeds the warnings of their children. Long-standing roles don't change easily, at least not without outside intervention. That's where the CHP finally stepped in and put an end to his reckless road trips.

My dad was driving back from Vegas and stopped at a Bun Boy coffee shop in Barstow. He missed the driveway entrance by a good ten feet, went up over the sidewalk, and came to a stop in front of a CHP officer sitting in his car eating lunch. Dad's driver's license was promptly revoked, which was a good thing. The downside was his morale and health declined quickly.

He succumbed to his illnesses after living with us for three years. It was a very difficult thing, taking care of a parent at home, but it also had a silver lining. My kids, Spencer and Hailey, spent a lot of hours with their grandpa that they wouldn't have had otherwise. I was grateful that he lived long enough to see my career start to turn around. I know he feared that might not happen. He was a pessimist to the end.

CHAPTER 47

Nerd in the New Millennium

The twentieth century was nearing an end. I was in my fourth decade of acting and still picking up momentum, booking television roles on *The Nanny*, *Ally McBeal*, *Sliders*, *Boston Common*, and a slew of movies for the Hallmark Channel. Some of these projects were quite good, others were not. That's the curse of a journeyman actor: you don't have the luxury of picking and choosing your work like Brad Pitt. Sometimes you wind up in a real stinker, being grateful just to be employed. Case in point: a miniseries titled *Final Approach*. It was an "airplane in distress" story and about as realistic as John Wayne playing Genghis Khan. I recommend catching this epic in reruns for its unintended comedic moments. I play a passenger, an aeronautical engineer (just like Steve Douglas), and Dean Cain is my seatmate, a disgraced FBI agent. Once we vanquish the hijackers, I'm forced to take control of our Boeing 747 since the pilots have been killed. My character has never flown a plane before but somehow manages to land the damaged jumbo jet on a desert airstrip that's about the size of a postage stamp. It was akin to dragging a rookie nurse into an operating room to single-handedly perform open-heart surgery. I suppose it didn't hurt to have Superman as my copilot. Sorry, Dean.

My musical side had an unexpected renaissance in the new millennium, too.

I was sorting cassette tapes in my office one day, and I came across an unmarked one. I put it into the player and was surprised to hear Karen singing a song titled "It Always Sounds Good." It was a rough demo and obviously a tune that she was writing. The lyrics were about a spouse considering a relationship with a former lover. That really piqued my curiosity. Since she had kept her vocal talents secret, I wondered if her lyrics were about a hidden affair as well. We'd always had a great marriage—honest, passionate, and full of laughter—so I approached her with the evidence (the tape).

Karen admitted that she was writing the song and that it was autobiographical. She also pointed out that the hero of her little ditty didn't succumb to temptation as the song's title, "It Always Sounds Good", suggests. Her logic put my paranoia to bed.

We embarked on a musical career as a singing duo, with me playing guitar, one of my lifelong passions. It was fun and exciting, especially since we had been married for fifteen years. Every longtime relationship occasionally needs a boost, and this was a perfect one for us. I began writing songs for us to perform, too. One of my better efforts was a humorous story song titled "Pretzel on the Rug." It was based on an unusual, albeit traumatic, experience I had at the White House. Let me digress . . .

I was in Washington, D.C., doing publicity for a project, and was introduced to a woman who worked at the White House in public relations. She said that President Bill Clinton was a big fan of *My Three Sons*, and she arranged for a private tour of the West Wing when it was officially closed, Sunday evening.

Karen and I and the kids showed up as planned, and a guide escorted us on a walking tour of the White House kitchen, the Rose Garden, the Press Room, even the basement where the foundation for the first mansion still exists; the masonry footings still show the black burn marks after the British torched the place in 1814.

We arrived at the Oval Office at ten in the evening, far past Spencer and Hailey's bedtimes. I came prepared, though, with a pocket full of pretzels hoping to keep the kids fueled up. Our guide gently swung open the office's curved door, revealing the president's private sanctuary. The Oval Office was the coolest stop on the tour. Spencer, who was seven at the time, was disinterested. He was worn out and starting to whine, so I slipped him a big pretzel to keep him occupied.

We stood in the doorway, behind a blue velvet rope, gazing at the inner sanctum of the most powerful man on earth. There was so much history that you could feel: Nixon plotting Watergate, Roosevelt plotting World War II, Clinton plotting his next (fill in the blank). I glanced down at Spencer to see if he was taking in this special moment just as he bit down on his pretzel.

To my horror, a large curled section, the part hanging from his mouth, snapped off and took flight like a Scud missile. Its trajectory sent it flying straight into the Oval Office, where it landed on the plush yellow carpet. It was about three feet into the room, within my reach, but my mind raced with concerns: *Should I reach over the velvet rope and pick it up? No, I better not because our guide said to stay behind the velvet rope. Do not enter the room, under any circumstances.*

I furtively glanced around; nobody noticed what had happened. Even Spencer was oblivious; he was more interested in licking the salt off his fingers. Once again my attention was drawn back to the offending pretzel on the rug. I couldn't take my eyes off it. It's like nothing else existed in the room except for that brown, curvy piece of junk food. A little voice in my head spoke up: *"It is just a pretzel, no big deal. Forget about it!"*

Our guide closed the curved door and that, mercifully, ended my moral crisis . . . or so I thought.

We continued our tour, walking down the hall for a peek into the Chief of Staff's office, and Spencer's whining began again. Without thinking, I whipped another pretzel out of my pocket. Before I could hand it to my son, two secret service agents grabbed me like I was Squeaky Fromme back for another assassination attempt. They literally pinned me to the wall and pried the crusty hunk of fried dough from my hand like it was a revolver.

"Did you throw a pretzel in the Oval Office?" one of the agents sneered.

I was dumbstruck and sputtered, "I . . . Huh? . . . Well . . . it . . . uh . . ."

"Did you?!" the other agent demanded. He was more determined to extract a confession than his partner.

I considered telling them the truth, which would have put the blame on my son. Then an Orwellian fear stopped me. *This kind of incident might go on a permanent record somewhere.* I decided to take the rap instead of exposing the true culprit, Spencer. He could be haunted by such an episode for the rest of his life knowing how wacky the government can be.

I whimpered, "It was an accident. It broke off and flew into the room. I didn't want to reach over . . ."

The first agent waved the pretzel in my face and growled, "You're not allowed to bring snack food in here. This isn't the city zoo, you're at the White House!"

I nodded with shame, accepting my traitorous act and emptying my pockets of pretzels.

The agents still weren't satisfied and gave me a quick patdown, making sure I didn't have a few Fig Newtons stashed in my underwear. They finally concluded that I was *clean* and shooed me away with disapproving scowls.

Later that night, after the tour, the family and I deduced that the Oval Office must be full of high-tech sensors that can detect foreign objects left in the room, things like listening devices or tiny explosives. We were impressed. It was very James Bond. Here are the lyrics to the song I wrote about the experience:

Pretzel on the Rug

Nobody touch it
It might explode
How it got here
Nobody knows
We're the secret service
Today we found a bug
In the Oval Office
There's a pretzel on the rug

Maybe it's a camera
With a microphone and lens
To catch our private conversations
And our sneaky little plans
Probably planted
By a third world thug
In the Oval Office
There's a pretzel on the rug

Don't take chances
Always fear the worst
The last man standing
Is the one who shoots first
Assassins and rivals
Are usually hid
Behind the face
Of a junk food eating kid

Call the bomb squad
Get that danger loving man
Bring the robot
With its ever-steady hand
Lift it lightly

It might be a deadly drug
In the Oval Office
There's a pretzel on the rug

Don't take chances
Always fear the worst
The last man standing
Is the one who shoots first
Assassins and rivals
Are usually hid
Behind the face
Of a junk food eating kid

So they took it to the lab
Here's what they found
Flour and salt
Cooked golden brown
Made by Nabisco
A snack that we all dug
In the Oval Office
There was a pretzel on the rug

There is a strange coda to this story. A few years after our visit, President George W. Bush actually choked on a pretzel. The incident made headlines because he nearly keeled over and died. I couldn't help wondering if a second hunk of Spencer's pretzel flew into the room and eluded the secret service's high-tech sensors. President Bush might have accidentally found that piece of junk food under a sofa, popped it in his mouth, and gagged. It's just a thought.

CHAPTER 48

A *My Three Sons* Movie?

 There is one question that fans ask most frequently: "Will there ever be a movie based on *My Three Sons?*" I don't think so, not with the remaining original cast members, anyway. Too many key people have passed on. There's always the possibility that it might get an "update," remade as a feature film. The show is certainly a brand name, something that studios are fixated on these days.

An updated version of *MTS* almost got made in 2002 when Michael Douglas was interested in producing it. I first learned about the project by reading an article in the *Dailey Variety*. It said that Douglas was developing a script and that he planned to star in the film playing Steve Douglas, the MacMurray role. Not a bad idea.

Michael Douglas was skilled in comedy and drama, just like MacMurray was. In fact, I saw a few more interesting parallels. Both actors had become huge film stars playing romantic cads in steamy potboilers (MacMurray in *Double Indemnity* and *The Apartment* and Douglas in *Basic Instinct* and *Fatal Attraction*). Both men were in their forties when they starred in their respective classic films. When MacMurray hit his fifties, and his days as a romantic lead were waning, he opted to play Steve Douglas, the eternally wholesome father. My guess is that Douglas, also now in his fifties, was at a similar crossroads regarding age and screen opportunities. *MTS* would have been a perfect vehicle for Douglas to find a new career niche. It's all speculation on my part.

About a year after I read the article, I finally found out what happened with the project while guest-starring on the series, *Will & Grace.* Michael Douglas was also in the episode (playing a gay detective and nominated for an Emmy), so I got it straight from the source.

All through the *Will & Grace* rehearsals, I waited for the right opportunity to quiz Michael about his version of *MTS.* I was a bit hesitant, though. I wasn't even sure if he knew that I was an original cast member. He gave no indication that he remembered me from the series. I wasn't even sure if he knew that we'd met twenty-five years earlier on his TV show, *The Streets of San Francisco.*

A quiet moment finally presented itself. I sat next to him and said, "Hey, Michael, I heard you were planning to do *My Three Sons* as a movie. You knew that I was on that series, right?"

He quickly replied, "Sure, sure I knew that!"

I wasn't so sure that was the truth. It seemed kind of strange for him to not mention it, particularly since I was somebody intimately connected with the show. Maybe he thought I might ask for a job. In any case, I posed the next obvious question. "So, are you going to do it?"

"Well . . . probably not." He sighed. "We're still trying to get the script right."

"What do you mean?" I said.

"It's been hard finding the right tone. We want to be true to the show's original feeling, which was pretty "La-la-land in Pleasantville," because we don't want to put off the old fans. Then, again, younger audiences today expect kids to have realistic problems, and those are pretty rough: drugs, pregnancies, school violence. The writers haven't found a way to bring those two worlds together yet. It looks like it's not going to happen."

Damn. I probably would have hit him up for a job, too.

All in all, though, Douglas's comments were savvy as hell. I think he made the right choice about not updating *My Three Sons* and letting it remain a warm, fuzzy TV memory.

CHAPTER 49

Embracing Ernie

As I grew older, I began to accept, even love, Ernie. I had amassed a good body of work post- *MTS*, and that put the little bugger in perspective: Ernie was just a role I had played, not the *only* role I had played. In my mind, I was the child actor who escaped the dubious has-been label. Of course, that's not how the producers of *Dickie Roberts, Former Child Star* saw me. They were rounding up the usual suspects (Jerry Mathers, Ron Pallilo, Todd Bridges, Gary Coleman, Willie Aames, etc.) to be in the film and poke fun at our pasts. I was also asked to participate and balked at the offer.

The theme of that movie focused on Dickie Roberts, a ficti- tious child star, who is now an adult has-been. The media loves to promote that myth, even if it's a big stretch of the truth. Ex– child stars implode in public once in a while, but it's far from the norm. The vast majority of professional kid actors go on to lead normal adult lives. It does make for juicy sound bites on *TMZ* , though, when someone hits the wall.

I had to think long and hard about associating myself with the film, even though it was only a cameo at the end. Thoughts swirled in my head: *I've done some great work lately, in most of the best shows on TV. Do I really want to be part of a film that's going to make fun of who I am? Aren't I trying to escape the past and not reinforce the old image?*

Then, another voice in my head spoke up: *Who am I kidding? No matter how many Oscars may be in my future, Ernie Douglas will be etched somewhere on my tombstone. If you can't fight them, join them.*

Filming took place at Paramount Studios, one of my favorite playgrounds as a kid. I was part of a chorus of child actors singing at the end of the movie. The saving grace was the song we sang, *Child Stars on Your Television*. It was a witty lament about the pain of being haunted by our famous alter egos. My solo verse went like this: "Don't ever say: Didn't you *use to be* ? Or I'll put your head through a vintage TV!" I could relate.

After the film came out, I continued working in hit shows like *The Drew Carey Show, Crossing Jordan,* and *Strong Medicine* (another recurring role as a doctor). It didn't hamper my new image one bit. In fact, had I not done *Dickie Roberts,* I would never have connected with Adam Sandler, the film's producer. A chance meeting with him eventually led to a choice role in one of his future films.

I was on the Sony Pictures lot doing an episode of *The Guardian* and decided to kill a little free time by walking over to the Happy Madison offices (Sandler's company). As always, I was in search of past employers and future work. Unfortunately, the place was deserted; everybody had gone to lunch, so I left. Nothing ventured, nothing gained.

I walked back outside just as a golf cart skidded to a stop in front of the offices, and Sandler hopped out of the driver's seat. He was in gym clothes and dripping with sweat, like he'd just come from a workout. For those of you who haven't been keeping track, Sandler has had more hit films than any other star in Hollywood over the past twenty years. He not only makes his own successful films, his company produces hits for other stars, too. The man is an industry titan and one of the most well-loved people in a town full of scoundrels.

He was hurrying to his offices as our eyes met. I said, "Hi,

Adam. I was in *Dickie Roberts,* the film you produced. You might remember me. I used to play Ernie Douglas on . . ."

"My Three Sons!" Sandler blurted out. "That was one of my favorite shows! Every night it was on, our whole family would gather in the living room and watch the show together!"

Sandler went on to recite the plots of his favorite episodes and saying how cool it was to meet me. It was pretty goddamn cool to meet him, too. What a genuinely nice guy.

Before parting ways, I thought I'd throw out a pitch for a job. I said, "I really appreciate being in *Dickie Roberts,* but I'd like to be in one of your films."

"Sure! Sure! I'll put you in one of my films, no problem!" Sandler replied.

Over the next four years, I auditioned for every Sandler movie that he was about to make. It wasn't my agent getting me through the door, either. It was Sandler telling his casting director to bring me in. He was holding true to his word.

I didn't book any of those jobs, probably because I wasn't the right type for the role. Regardless, I was blown away that such an industry mogul, a man with a thousand details a day to attend to, would remember our short conversation. What a guy. He eventually kept his promise.

CHAPTER 50

More Top Secret Projects

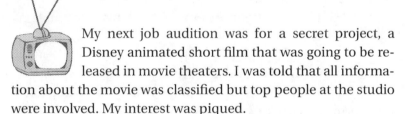 My next job audition was for a secret project, a Disney animated short film that was going to be released in movie theaters. I was told that all information about the movie was classified but top people at the studio were involved. My interest was piqued.

I went to the audition and waited in a big room with all the other balding, academic types. A casting assistant finally led me into the office to read for the film's director, Forest Whitaker. There are a few modern actors whose work I really admire: Jack Nicholson, Meryl Streep, Johnny Depp, Robert Duvall, and Forest Whitaker. He is the type of actor I aspire to be: versatile, passionate, and committed to his craft.

Whitaker divulged that Disney hired him to make a live-action introduction to an animated short film, *The Legend of John Henry*. The animated part of the project was already completed. He described it as a "labor of love" by a group of prominent studio artists headed by Roy Disney.

I read for the part of a teacher lecturing his class about John Henry, the mythological black railroad worker who could tunnel faster than a machine. After I got the role, I learned why the project was swirling in secrecy and controversy.

Apparently, some executives at Disney got cold feet about releasing a film about an African American legend because a

236

predominately Caucasian production team produced it. They feared a critical backlash in the black community, no matter how "Oscar worthy" the animation was. The movie had become a stealth project, a labor of love but too risky to release or show anyone.

The executives hired Forest Whitaker to salvage the film, hoping his participation, no matter how incidental to the animated section, would deflect any criticism. Disney is very, very cautious with their brand name and will go to great lengths to avoid controversy.

Whitaker shot a beautiful introduction where my teacher character scoffs at the notion that man, no matter what his color or strength, could beat a machine.

The nervous executives saw the finished project and still feared a high-profile slap in the face. *The Legend of John Henry*, the supposedly Oscar-worthy short film, went straight to video, minus my scene, too. I was pretty disappointed. I do feel that things happen for a reason, though, because something unexpected and wonderful came out of this job about a year later.

I was having dinner with good friend Bob Hummer and his wife, Dawn, on a Friday night, and my cell phone rang. It was my agent calling.

"You just got hired on a major studio film. It's called *First Daughter*. Congratulations!" he said.

"Huh? . . . What?" I stammered.

"*First Daughter*, it's a Fox film starring Katie Holmes and Michael Keaton. You're on it for four weeks!" he replied.

"You're kidding?" I gasped. This job came totally out of the blue, no first audition, no callbacks, nothing. "Who's the director?"

"Forest Whitaker," he said.

Snap!

I started work the very next Monday playing the press secretary to Keaton's president. Forest is one of America's best actors and a helluva director, too.

Following my work on *First Daughter*, my commercial agent sent me on another top-secret audition. This was becoming an intriguing habit. I was to meet with a casting director, Laray Mayfield, for a Heineken beer spot. Nothing more could be revealed.

I went on the interview in the afternoon and booked the job that evening. No callback, again! That was highly unusual. Commercials *always* have callbacks. Actors must be paraded before a committee of advertising people so they can determine if you are the right person to sell their toilet paper. It's akin to brain surgery.

I couldn't believe my luck when my agent said that my commercial was going to air during the Super Bowl. They are the crème de la crème of advertising. Not only that, the spot was going to be directed by David Fincher! Fincher was at the helm of some of my favorite films: *Fight Club, Panic Room*, and *Seven*. Advertising agencies spare no expense for their Super Bowl spots. Bragging rights are at stake.

I reported to work in downtown Los Angeles about a week later, excited to meet Fincher and play my part in the hush-hush commercial. I was told only one thing about my role: I was going to play a doorman at an exclusive condo and work with another actor. After donning my wardrobe, a company van ferried me to the set where I met the other actor: Brad Pitt. Brad Pitt?! Wow, this job really took an unexpectedly cool turn.

I was just a supporting player in the commercial whose story had Brad Pitt, mega–movie star, eluding fans and paparazzi as he hunts for a cold Heineken.

We were introduced, and Pitt said, "Hey, man, I should say *Hi, Barry* when I see you. You're my doorman, right? We probably talk from time to time, don't you think?"

Pitt's simple suggestion spoke volumes about his generosity as an actor. He put me on an equal footing as a collaborator, making the scene more believable. Trust me, I've worked with plenty of stars who don't give supporting players squat. They take the bucks and run, particularly in a commercial. Brad Pitt is worth a million in my book. In fact, I heard he made a few million for that commercial. They pay you what you are worth in Hollywood.

CHAPTER 51

Working with Future Legends

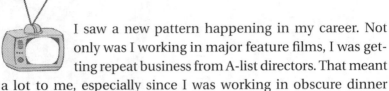 I saw a new pattern happening in my career. Not only was I working in major feature films, I was getting repeat business from A-list directors. That meant a lot to me, especially since I was working in obscure dinner theater not that long ago. All the hard work, the networking, sending out flyers, acting in small theater productions, seemed to help get my career back on track. I was on a roll.

After the Heineken commercial, my agent called me and said, "David Fincher is looking for a really good actor to play a newspaper editor in his next film, *Zodiac*. There's no scripted dialogue at the moment, but there'll be plenty of opportunities to improvise some things. It's four weeks' work. Interested?"

Hell, yeah! What actor is going to say no to working with David Fincher again, not to mention getting the chance to rub elbows with Robert Downey Jr., Jake Gyllenhaal, and Mark Ruffalo? Not I.

Over the next four weeks, Fincher asked me to improvise dialogue in a few scenes. Unfortunately, it didn't make it into the final cut. No hard feelings, though. The film is almost three hours long and my verbal additions were hardly critical to the plot. That being said, *Zodiac* is a brilliantly complex piece of filmmaking. It is an absolute classic, and I got a front-row seat watching it get made.

David Fincher is the most exacting director I've ever worked with. He knows where the camera should be at all times and how it should move. He is also precise in what he wants from an actor's performance. That can translate into many, many takes of the same scene. I found his process to be no problem because Fincher's requests were concise and understandable. As long as the director has a specific change in mind, and conveys it clearly, I'll do the scene forty times without getting uptight. Things get dicey when a director asks you to do it again and says *be funnier* or *speed it up*. That kind of direction is so vague it's easy to get confused and frustrated; that's a scary place for an actor to be.

From my close-up vantage point, Robert Downey Jr. seemed to be the actor most stressed by Fincher's requests for multiple takes. He is a performer who thrives on spontaneity. Repetition can sometimes lead to stagnation for such quicksilver artists. After the twentieth take (occasionally more), Downey would look at me and quietly roll his eyes from fatigue. Being the consummate professional, though, he never lost his cool and dove back into the next take, trying to match Fincher's requests for new shadings. The man is the John Coltrane of jazz acting.

In the final cut, Downey's performance as a brilliant man who falls victim to his own vices, is as good as it gets. What you see on screen is Fincher's talent for molding Downey's mercurial skills into a stellar performance. I am such a fan of both men.

There were other challenges we faced while filming *Zodiac*. Our sprawling set, duplicating the *San Francisco Chronicle*'s offices, was constructed on the fourth floor of the old Terminal Annex Building in downtown Los Angeles. The nearest bathroom was on the first floor and accessed by a maddeningly slow elevator. You didn't dare leave the set to go to the toilet, because it took so damn long to make the journey, let alone "do" your business. Believe me, the last thing you want to see upon your return is everybody standing around waiting for you. Not a good way to endear yourself to the director. Come to think of it, I don't know that I ever saw Fincher leave the set to relieve himself. The man must have a camel-size bladder, a big plus when you're driving a film that cost sixty-five million dollars to make.

Robert Downey Jr., on the other hand, must have had a normal-size bladder like the rest of us mortals. He resorted to sneaking off whenever possible into the building's dark corners to pee into a large coffee can. One day he made an announcement: "If you ever find a coffee can with my name written on it with a blue Sharpie, it's not full of Yuban. It's my personal Porta Potty."

Late one night, after shooting had wrapped after a long day, a relieved-looking Downey emerged from the back of the building. I saw he was toting his can and watched him discreetly toss it into a Dumpster. I said, "Robert, you shouldn't throw that away. Put it up for auction on eBay. You could probably get a lot of money for it."

Downey laughed, knowing I was joking about celebrities who sell their useless crap online. He said, "You're right! I could probably sell it. It wouldn't be worth anything, though, it's drug-free." He's a funny guy with a huge talent, very resourceful, too.

After *Zodiac* wrapped, I was asked to audition for a new series, *Mad Men*, which chronicled the exploits of Madison Avenue advertising men in the 1960s. I had a connection to that world through my Uncle Bernard who worked at one of the big agencies during that era.

When I met with Matt Weiner, the show's creator/producer, I told him about my uncle's favorite activity: taking afternoon naps. After lunchtime cocktails with "the boys," he'd return to his office, close the blinds, lock his door, and take a nice, long snooze. He had no qualms about his lousy work ethic, either. He was a lifelong member of the Communist Party, so working on Madison Avenue was a big compromise to his proletariat principles. He used to say, "I earned my living on Madison Avenue, working in the belly of the capitalist beast. Naps were just my way of saying, 'fuck you' to the whole corrupt system!" He was quite a colorful guy.

Matt Weiner enjoyed hearing about my uncle's distaste for Mad Avenue. He also liked my reading and hired me to play one of "the lecherous guys" in the art department, Duane Davis. It was another new kind of character, far from my famous alter ego, Ernie Douglas, who seemed to be a vague memory to one and all now.

Over time, I'd grown accustomed to going unrecognized for being on *My Three Sons*. On rare occasions somebody on a set would ask: "Didn't you used to be . . ." And that was fine. I'd readily 'fess up. I wasn't trying to hide the fact, but I just wasn't going to promote it, either. As the Beatles sang: *Let it be.*

My work on *Mad Men* required me to do some period dancing, the Twist and the Cha-Cha, in a bar scene. Dance rehearsals commenced with all of the show's principals. I could tell that none of the show's young stars had an inkling about who I "used to be." Fine by me. I was just another actor on their show that week—politely ignored. That's standard behavior on most every set. The stars huddle in their clique, and the supporting players gather in their corner. No big deal.

After a while, Matt Weiner, the show's creator and King of the Realm, came down to watch rehearsals. When the King is on the set, all of the series regulars are on high alert, secretly hoping for his attention. After all, he's responsible for writing your role and can make or break your career. We supporting actors are hopeful for acknowledgment, too, but it's not likely going to happen. The day players are just a tiny blip on the producer's busy radar screen.

After we showed Weiner our dance moves, he shared a few hushed words with the choreographer and headed for the exit, all eyes following his every step. As he passed by me, though, he abruptly paused, clasped my arm, and whispered, "I know who you are." Then the King dashed out through the door.

I glanced back at my fellow actors, stars and day players alike. Their puzzled eyes were fixed upon me. It was easy to read their funny expressions: "So . . . who the hell *is* he, anyway?"

Soon after, word spread like wildfire that I was someone who used to be famous, and the stars welcomed me into their exclusive club. So much for anonymity. The TV ghosts from *My Three Sons* are here forever, I suppose.

Over time, I began to think that being Ernie wasn't such a bad thing, especially since I got another request to come read for a role in Adam Sandler's next film, *You Don't Mess with the Zohan*. I'd auditioned for every one of his films since we met four years earlier. Sandler was really proving himself to be a huge and loyal fan of *My Three Sons*.

My audition was for the character of Gray Kleibolt, a corporate toady out to destroy the Zohan. I prepped hard for the interview, even enlisting the advice of my friend and mentor, Steve Railsback. The reading with the casting director, Randi Hiller, went well, and I kept my fingers crossed.

Weeks went by, and I heard nothing. As Tom Petty aptly sang: "*The waiting is the hardest part.*" At last, I got a call requesting that I attend a "table read" of the script. My agent told me very clearly that I didn't have the part yet. That statement was unnerving, mainly because a table read is just that: a simple recitation of the script for the director and writer to hear the words, no acting allowed. Since I didn't have the role, this put me in a bit of a bind: if my reading were flat, I'd run the danger of looking boring and not being cast. On the other hand, if I read with too much gusto, I'd look like a big ham and lose the role. It was thin ice either way.

The day of the table read arrived, and I went to a huge conference room at Sony Studios. It was packed with actors, writers, studio executives, wives, and girlfriends. I found an open chair, took a breath, and reminded myself: *Listen and react, listen and react, keep it simple.* A hand tapped me on the shoulder, snapping me out of my meditation. I turned to see Sandler standing behind me, grinning. "Hey, Barry, I told you I'd get you something good! I told you, didn't I?" he said.

I practically wept.

I read my part, and it went great, nailing the jokes that the writers had given my character. I got up to leave and spied Sandler across the room, surrounded by his "people." I was hoping for a little eye contact, but I got a helluva lot more than that. Sandler waved and yelled, "Good job, Barry! Thanks, man!"

It's always a good thing to have an industry titan complimenting you in front of the studio executives. I was finally cast in one of his movies, just like he had promised.

I hate to get slavish singing the praises of Sandler, but his unique character warrants testimony. I worked on *Zohan* for four weeks, and I can tell you that there isn't an ounce of pretension or bullshit in him. If he saw a production assistant hunting for a place to sit at lunch, he'd make room for him at his table. If he was lighting up an expensive Havana cigar and saw you watching him, he'd offer you one. I casually mentioned that my son Spencer had a band called the Alternates. Months after this conversation, I took my son to the Happy Madison Christmas party. When Adam arrived, he picked us out of the crowd, rushed over, stuck out his hand to my son, and said, "You must be Spencer. How's the band doing?" Again, I held back a tear. What a mensch.

CHAPTER 52

Big Love

 If *My Three Sons* depicted the most wholesome family in TV history, then the HBO series, *Big Love*, wins the medal for presenting the most amoral clan. It's a wonderfully warped universe of polygamy, treachery, and deception. I was thrilled that my next job was a recurring role on the series playing the lawyer who represents the show's lecherous church leader, Roman Grant. I defended him at his big child-molestation rape trial. It doesn't get much juicer than that.

The show boasts a galaxy of talented stars such as Bill Paxton, Jeanne Tripplehorn, Bruce Dern, and Ellen Burstyn, to name a few. I had the good fortune to spend most of my time acting with Harry Dean Stanton who plays the sinister family patriarch.

Stanton, for those of you who don't know, is a Hollywood outlaw icon and a mentor to people like Sean Penn, Tim Robbins, and his old roommate, Jack Nicholson. I was happy to learn that Stanton, now over eighty years old, hasn't forsaken his wild ways. He goes out drinking every night, whether he has to be on the set at six in the morning or not. Despite his all-night carousing, I never saw him miss a mark or muff a line of dialogue.

Stanton's not the most open, gregarious guy you'll ever meet, but, eventually, we connected on music. Years before our meeting, I saw him onstage at a Los Angeles nightclub, the Mint, singing his beloved Mexican folk songs in a clear high tenor. He was authentic and terrific, and I told him so. My praise warmed the thorny old outlaw up, and he asked me if I'd been acting for long.

I said, "Harry, if there's one person on this set who's been acting longer than you have, it's me." That got his attention. We determined that he had me beat by four years. His earliest job was in 1954, in a TV show called *Inner Sanctum*. My first job was *Rally 'Round the Flag, Boys!* in 1958. I told Stanton that I was on *My Three Sons* and asked him if he ever did an episode.

He thought for a moment, rubbing his gray gaunt face, and then said blankly, "I've never heard of the show." I should have guessed.

CHAPTER 53

The Social Network

 The biggest new project in my long and winding career hit the movie theaters in 2010, *The Social Network*, directed by David Fincher. This is the fourth time I've worked with him (*Zodiac* and two commercials, Heineken and Orville Redenbacher popcorn). What a pleasure to be part of his creative world. The film was nominated for numerous awards and won Best Picture at the Golden Globes and three Academy Awards on Oscar night.

In addition to Fincher, the film was loaded with talent. Aaron Sorkin, author of *A Few Good Men* and creator of *West Wing*, wrote the script, and Jesse Eisenberg, star of *The Squid and the Whale* and *Zombieland*, and singer/actor Justin Timberlake headline the cast.

Sorkin's screenplay is an adaptation of a book, *The Accidental Billionaires*. It's about the genius nerds (my kind of people) at Harvard who created the Internet sensation, Facebook. It's a fascinating look at the lives of these young and brilliant young men. They are the Thomas Edisons of our age, and very few people were aware of their story.

I play Harvard's computer security chief, an older nerd named Cox, who has to deal with the shenanigans of the computer geeks running amok on campus.

During the shooting of the film, Fincher was his usual self: a relentless perfectionist. Example: my first scene (Cox being awakened in the middle of the night by a phone call) required at least twenty-five takes. Sometimes he'd ask me to try different line readings, sometimes the camera moved incorrectly, a few times we repeated the scene because my "wife," in the background and asleep, didn't look relaxed enough. Fincher has the eyes and ears of an eagle; nothing escapes his attention. I would have repeated the scene another twenty-five times if he'd asked for it because I knew in the end he'd make my work look as good as it can get. What more can you ask for?

Old nerds, young nerds, they're everywhere you look in this film. The amazing thing is that they have become today's rock stars, in film and in real life. Who could have guessed? I started out playing them as a boy and continue to do as a grown man, which leads me to believe that there are no endings, only new beginnings.

Back to the Autograph Show

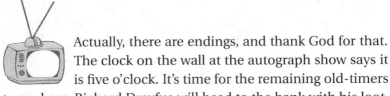Actually, there are endings, and thank God for that. The clock on the wall at the autograph show says it is five o'clock. It's time for the remaining old-timers to pack up. Richard Dreyfus will head to the bank with his loot, Jay North is on his way back to his prison job, and I'm going home to be with the wife and kids.

We're up to date as far as my career goes. And I haven't had an acting job for six months now. Uh-oh. Could I be on the downslide again? Anything is possible, as I've learned. You know what else I've learned? I can cope with the ups and the downs. I may not resurface for another twenty years . . . when they finally remake *My Three Sons* and I'll be cast as crusty old Uncle Charley.

The acting business is a weird, wonderful world. It has taken me on a long, eventful ride. I started out strong as a youngster with *My Three Sons,* worked on stages from Broadway to Salt Lake City, went into a midlife career hibernation, battled some demons, started a family, became Mr. Mom, and began a slow, tenacious climb back into a respectable adult acting career.

I can't wait to see what's coming next. Because I'm not going away any time soon.

Acknowledgments

I'd like to give thanks to the people who, directly or indirectly, enriched my life and helped bring this book to life:

My brother, Stanley Livingston; my editor at Kensington Books, Gary Goldstein; my agent, Al Zuckerman; Dr. Philip Hawley Jr., Robert Hummer, Paul Jackson, Chris Craven, Mitch Gelman, Hailey Livingston, Spencer Livingston, Brent Maddock, David Nelson, Sam Nelson, Penny Perry, Laray Mayfield, Michael Zanuck, Pam Sparks, Lynda McCarrell, Lorenzo Hodges, Lorra-Lee Bartlett, Dierdre Baxter, Mike Lanigan, David O'Malley, John Stephens, John Gilstrap, Nat Bernstein, Jack Lanigan, Mi-Jack, Inc., Randal Kleiser, Harry Flynn, Bill Paxton, Richard LeRoy, Perry Herwood, Maureen Herwood, Bill Livingston, Corine Livingston, Michelle Shepherd, John Shepherd, Tony Blake, Sherilyn Jackson, Scott Spiegel, and Forest Whitaker.

Index

Printed in the United States
by Baker & Taylor Publisher Services